LANGUAGE AND LANGUAGES

Derek Strange

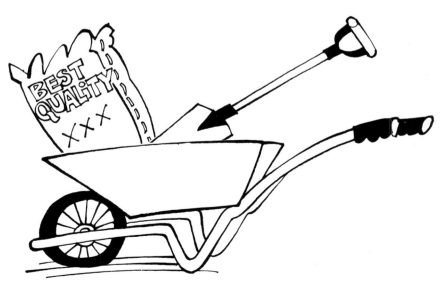

Oxford University Press

Oxford University Press, Walton Street, Oxford OX2 6DP

Oxford New York Toronto
Delhi Bombay Calcutta Madras Karachi
Petaling Jaya Singapore Hong Kong Tokyo
Nairobi Dar es Salaam Cape Town
Melbourne Auckland

and associated companies in
Beirut Berlin Ibadan Nicosia

Oxford is a trade mark of Oxford University Press

ISBN 0 19 912051 X

Acknowledgements

Photographs courtesy of Camera Press, John Topham Picture Agency
and the Royal National Institute for the Deaf.

Illustrations by Marie-Hélène Jeeves, calligraphy by Nicky While.

To my parents

Set by Rowland Phototypesetting Ltd,
Bury St Edmunds, Suffolk
Printed in Hong Kong

CONTENTS

INTRODUCTION FOR THE TEACHER

This book is designed for pupils who are about to begin learning a foreign language. It aims to develop the pupils' awareness of language, and to encourage them to think about ways of listening to and looking at the second language they are going to study. This of course involves thinking about their mother tongue too. Some basic methods of linguistic analysis are introduced and exercised unit by unit.

The content of the units can be outlined as follows:

Unit 1 An introductory overview of some of the different living languages of the world. Making language sounds. Some different ways of writing down languages. Roots, evolutions, and similarities of main world language groups.

Unit 2 Pieces of sound and pieces of meaning: words and pieces of words seen as the basic 'bricks' out of which the language 'house' is built.

Unit 3 The different kinds of plan used to build sentences. Plans for speaking: building 'language-walls'. Ways of making longer or shorter sentences without changing the basic (grammatical) plan.

Unit 4 Plans for meanings. The possibility of conveying meanings without conventional language: i.e. meaning on its own. Putting meanings into words. Different meanings in ambiguity.

Unit 5 Tones of voice, patterns of intonation and what they can mean. Importance of accent: accurate pronunciation. 'Styles' of speaking: different ways of conveying the same message to different people. Expressions and gestures that are commonly used to support meaning in language.

Unit 6 Some practical uses of learning a new language: language for a purpose. This unit can be linked directly to the pupils' own start on one particular second language.

It is estimated that one unit will take up two and a half to three hours of classroom time.

Some concepts and terms basic to language study, such as *word*, *sentence*, *gender*, *number*, *interrogative*, and *imperative*, are also explained and illustrated as simply as possible in this book. Some familiarity with such terms will make the pupils' later language study simpler and more interesting. These terms are therefore not skirted round here.

After each explanatory section in the units some activity-based practice is given. The activities are designed to let pupils start trying out parts of language systems of English and other languages *experimentally*. They are basic linguistic experiments which will improve the pupils' powers of observation and accuracy – both so vital to good second language learning and good use of English.

The length of the activities varies. Some are intended to be done in groups or as a whole class; some are best done as pair work; some are best done by pupils on their own. Pronunciation guides are given wherever some help seems needed with difficult foreign words and sounds. These can of course only provide approximations of the foreign sounds. They are based on the pronunciation system used in *The Oxford School Dictionary* and *The Oxford Intermediate Dictionary*.

The following symbols are used for the activities:

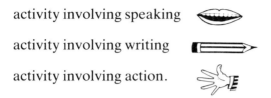

activity involving speaking

activity involving writing

activity involving action.

The activities can be extended and biased to suit the special second language(s) to be studied by pupils later. Extra examples from French, German, Spanish, or other 'school' languages can usefully be added. Children from bilingual backgrounds can also be encouraged to add information on their own languages wherever possible. Teachers can draw from other languages with which they are familiar, as appropriate. ·

At the end of each unit is a 'Things to discover' section. These are intended to provide some project work, which can be done either individually or in groups, associated with the work done in each unit. Such project work can be set as homework or for library studies at school, using atlases, encyclopaedias, larger dictionaries, and so on. For some of the project tasks the teacher may be asked to provide several copies of an atlas or dictionary, or to set up a tape-recorder for listening to pupils' recordings, or to act as a general informant as far as possible. The tasks are, however, meant to help the pupils to search, listen, and deduce for themselves. They can be extended to suit pupils' hobbies, to take in regional varieties of English accents, to encourage bilingual pupils' abilities, or to suit the teacher's own experience.

LANGUAGES PEOPLE LIVE WITH

The language palace and the mouth-machine

Have you ever thought about all the different languages that people use every day all over the world? Living in the world and speaking just one language is rather like living in an enormous palace and staying in only one room of it all the time. Learning other languages is like exploring the other rooms of your palace.

Even now, as you are reading these words, at least three to four *thousand* different languages are being spoken around the world. Some of the most important of these are English (and American or Australian or Canadian English), Spanish, Chinese, and French. These important languages are spoken by many millions of people. On the other hand, there are some languages which are spoken by only a few thousand or a few hundred people.

All these languages have some things in common though. Firstly, they all have the same main purpose. Why do people speak to each other or write to each other? Of course it is to give each other some kind of information, in other words to *communicate*, to send a message. Secondly, all languages when they are spoken are made by the same 'machine' – your voice and parts of your mouth. We will call this the 'mouth-machine'.

What do we know about this voice and mouth 'machine'? All sorts of different sounds and movements can be made by changing the position or shape of parts of your mouth, and most of these different sounds are used by one language or another (by one of the 3,000 or more languages in the world) to make up words and to *say* things to one another.

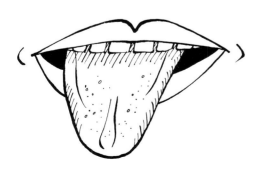

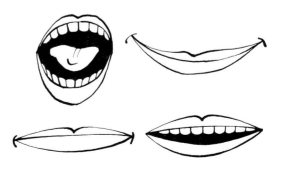

First there's the **tongue**, which wags up and down, and which you can stick out.

Then there are your **lips**, which you can open and close or smile with.

5

There are your **teeth**, which don't move (I hope), but which you use together with your tongue or lips when you make **th** and **f** sounds. Try it and you'll see.

Your **cheeks** are elastic and move around and change shape when your jaw moves up or down, but they don't actually help to *make* sounds or words.

Then there's the **'roof'** of your mouth, which stays still and is used together with the tip or the back of your tongue to make **k** or **sss** sounds, for example.

Then, going right to the back of your mouth, there are different parts of your throat that can make different sounds, and somewhere down there is your **'voice-box'** too. That's where the buzzing noise which you call your 'voice' comes from.

If you didn't have a voice-box you would have no voice and you'd only be able to whisper your words. We will see how we turn our voice-boxes on and off in the middle of lots of our words in English.

Last, but not least, there is the **nose**, which we use for making 'nose noises' like hummmming, for example. The **m** sound is one of the nose noises.

These are the most useful parts of the mouth-machine, used to make words in all the different languages of the world. The same machine can make over 3,000 different languages! That's some machine!

Now it's up to you to try out a few of the sounds you can make with all these parts of your mouth. Remember that because you speak English, you use lots of them every day without even thinking about it. Here, you will have to think about what you do every day in English.

Follow these instructions:

1 Say the words 'bumble bee' out loud. Now whisper them. Now say 'mother' out loud. Now whisper it. Now say 'Good old Bonzo' out loud. Now whisper it.

When you say things out loud your voice-box is turned on; when you whisper, it is turned off. If you put the tips of your fingers against your Adam's apple (the front of your throat), you can feel it buzzing when your voice-box is on, and not when it's off.

2 Stick your tongue out as far as possible. Can you see the end of it? How long do you think it is from your teeth to the end of it? Measure it if you can.

3 Bend the tip of your tongue up and try to touch your nose. Now down, and try to reach the bottom of your chin. Now bend it back into your mouth as far towards your throat as you can, and say 'ahh' while it is there.

You can see that you have very good control over your tongue. You can make it bend and stretch to exactly where you want in your mouth. That's why it is used to make so many different sounds in all the languages of the world.

4 Close your lips and hold your nose. Blow hard. Before you blow up completely, open your lips again a little bit, and let all the air rush out. What letter of the alphabet did it sound like as the air burst out through your lips? It should have been a **p** or a **b** sound.

5 Make a loud kissing noise. This is the same thing as letting the air rush *out* through your lips, except that now it will be rushing *in*. Some languages use this sound to make parts of their words. The Hottentots and Zulus in South Africa do, for example. Instead of the **t** sound in these words, make a quick kissing sound:

not, fight, letter, butter.

That's something like what some Zulu words sound like.

6 Spread your lips widely in a big smile, keeping your lips a little open. Now make a sound (voice-box turned on) without changing their shape at all and with your tongue flat on the bottom of your mouth. What letter of the alphabet does that sound like? Now make them as round and tight (but not closed) as possible. Make a sound again. And what's that letter?

7 Put your lower lip gently against the sharp edge of your top teeth, and blow air outwards. That's another letter of the alphabet. If you turn your voice-box on and off as you are doing this you can hear two different sounds of the alphabet – what are they? Now close your lips completely and hum. What letter of the alphabet is that? You see, your lips can be used to make all sorts of different sounds.

8 Put the tip of your tongue against the sharp edge of your front teeth, and blow outwards. Turn your voice-box on and off in short bursts as you do this, keeping your tongue against your teeth. You will be making two different **th** sounds. Try to find the 'voice-box *on*' sounds and the 'voice-box *off*' sounds in this sentence by saying it out loud a few times:

The **th**in **th**rush sat on **th**at **th**istle and was **th**rilled.

7

9 Now make a buzzing noise: **zzzz**. Where is the tip of your tongue now? And is your voice-box on or off? It must be *on*, mustn't it? Otherwise, if it was *off*, what sound would you hear?

10 Now pretend that you are gargling with water after brushing your teeth. Where are you making the sounds? Lots of sounds used in languages come from way back in your throat too.

You can stop and start the sounds made right down there too, as if someone has grabbed you by the throat in the middle of a word. Try stopping these words at the letter t, just for a second, and then finish saying the word:

better, bottle, nuts and bolts, kettle.

That's a bit like a London Cockney accent, isn't it?

You can do it!

Almost *any* sounds that you can think of making *comfortably* with all the different parts of your mouth-machine are actually being used somewhere in the world as bits of words, right now as you read. It is not only the kinds of sounds that we use every day to make English words that are used by other people to make their words. We all have the same mouth-machines to make sounds with, whether we are English, German, Russian, Spanish, or Chinese; so it must be possible for us to make other people's sounds properly by using *our own* mouth-machines in the right way.

Activity 2

1 Say these words out loud: **barber, bible, bubble, baby.**
Which parts of your mouth-machine are you using to make the **b** with? And is your voice-box on or off?

2 Try to say these German words: **Fritz, Fest, Feld, Fisch, Fleck, frisch.**
Which parts of your mouth-machine are you using to make the **f** sound? Can you make some English words using the same parts?

3 You should now be able to say these Spanish words: **flamenco, flor, fontana, fósforo, frontera.**
You can see that all three languages (English, German, and Spanish) use the same f sound in various words, and that the sound is made with exactly the same parts of your mouth-machine. Lots of other languages use exactly this same sound too.

4 What parts of your mouth do you use to make these English words? Try to say *how* you are using them (e.g. voice-box on/off, completely closed/open, etc.).
(a) gaggle, gurgle, giggle, goggle.
(b) mumble, mime, mum, mammal.
(c) little, label, lie, law, low.
(d) perhaps, pimple, poppy, pupil, peep.
(e) dad, did, dud, dead, died.

5 Here are some words that we use in English, taken from one of the languages of South-East Asia. Say them out loud, and you will see how easily we can make their words with our mouth-machines.

orangutan, kapok, paddy, bamboo.

If you don't already know, find out what these words mean when we use them in English.

Writing it down

We are now going to think about the ways in which languages can be written down. People all over the world may be able to make the sounds of spoken language by using the same sort of mouth-machine, but when it comes to writing things down, all sorts of different shapes and signs are used. Spoken language and written language are two quite separate things: a letter of our English alphabet may have a certain *sound* for us when we read it out, but a completely different *sound* for a French or German speaker when they read it out, and yet it is the same thing written down on paper. For example, the letter **i** makes us think of the sounds it has in words like **it** or **in** or **pip**, or else in words like **time**, **mine**, or **kite** in English. But a Spaniard would look at the letter **i** (written down) and would think of the **eee** sound that we use in words like **feet** and **teeth**. So in Spanish the word **fino** is said **'feeno'**.

So you can see that written language and spoken language are really two separate ways of sending a message. They are, in some ways, two different languages.

Look at these words, written down here, and try to think of the ways you would *say* them as English words. They may look the same and yet be said in different ways to mean different things. Or they may sound the same and yet be written down in different ways, which shows that they mean different things.

1 read, red, read
2 lead, led, lead (*metal*)
3 allowed, aloud
4 bow, bough, bow (*and arrow*)
5 prince, prints
6 plough, cough, dough, through
7 enough, puff, tough
8 (a) The sun's rays meet.
   (b) The sons raise meat.

From these words and sentences you will have been able to see and hear that there are important differences between spoken English and written English. Two words which you spell the same when you write them will not always sound the same; and all sorts of different letters can be used to write down the things people say and hear.

Activity 4 

There are many languages that do not even use the same kind of letters to write things down as we use in English. These languages have completely different alphabets. Russian and Greek are two European languages that have different alphabets from ours. And in other parts of the world there are different alphabets again.

Here are a few examples of the different alphabets that some languages use for writing things down.

1 Russian:

Что это ?
Это спутник

(What's that?
That's a sputnik.)

2 Chinese:

我是中国人

(I am a Chinaman.)

3 Hindi (Indian language):

वुम् और
बच्चा

(A woman and a child.)

4 Eskimo:

angutit ilât
iterssarssuarmut
arqapoq

(. . . one of them went into the cave . . .)

5 Zulu:

La la sithandwa
lal' uphumule

(Sleep, dear one, sleep and rest.)

6 Hebrew:

טְעִים
אֲבוֹ, תוֹרוּבִים

(Avocados are delicious.)

7 Cherokee (North American Indian):

ᏣᎩᎰᏑᎢ ᏭᏪᎪ
ᏒᏣᎩᏅᏣᎪ

(The Cherokees, when they were first discovered . . .)

8 Mohawk:

Onenh nonwa
oghseronnih
denighroghkwayen.

(Now then, let us
smoke the
pipe together.)

9 Arabic:

الله معاك

(God be with you.)

10 Japanese:

柔術

(jujitsu)

フッtボ ール

(football)

(a) First of all try to work out how you might say the words in numbers 4, 5, and 8.

(b) Now try to imagine how you would say numbers 2, 3, 6, and 9. You probably can't even guess what these letters should sound like, can you?

(c) Now try to copy out neatly onto paper the letters in numbers 2 and 3 or in numbers 7 and 10. You will find that it takes you a lot longer than it would to write down the same things in English.

(d) Here is the Russian alphabet. Use the Russian letters to write down your own name in Russian. You will see how different your name looks. In Russian there are no letters for C, H, Q, W or Y. If you need a C, H, Q, W or Y just use the English letters.

A = А Э	B = Б	D = Д	E = Е
F = Ф	G = Г	I = И, И	J = Ж
K = К	L = Л	M = М	N = Н
O = О	P = П	R = R	S = С
T = Т	U = У, Ю	V = В	X = Х
Their letters for our sounds: ts = Ц ch = Ч sh = Ш			Z = З

You can write down the names of some of your friends and family too.

(e) **Spy Game:** Divide into two teams. Each team has to think up a secret message, with the same number of words in it as there are people in the team. Each person writes down *one* of the words of the message *in code*, using the Russian alphabet as the code, on a small piece of paper. When both teams are completely ready, swap over the messages. The winning team will be the one that can decode the words and work out the whole message properly first.

The history of language

Where did so many different languages come from, so many different ways of making language-sounds with the same mouth-machine, and so many different ways of writing these sounds down? For a long way back in history people always seem to have spoken many different languages. If there was once one single language from which all other languages have come like a family tree, science has not been able to find any good proof of it.

One thing does seem certain. That is that some words have been 'borrowed' from one language by another. These words have travelled from one country and its language to another during invasions, and with traders and so on. Some of the words have changed slightly on their way. Look at the journey of our English word 'father', for example. Its journey into our modern English has taken hundreds of years, but now we use it every day. 'Father' is a lot older than you may have thought he was!

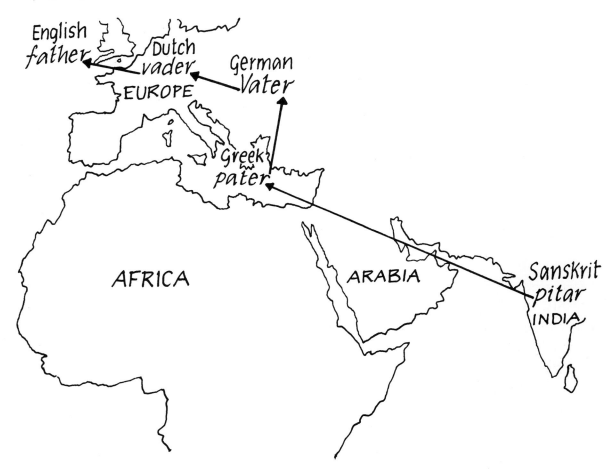

Links like this can be found not only between single words in different languages, but between whole languages. Languages can be grouped together, like the members of a family.

English belongs to the same huge language-family as French, Spanish, Italian, German, and many other modern, living languages. The family is called the **Indo-European** group. It is the biggest family of languages that there is in the world: about half of the people in the world speak a language which is a member of this huge language-family! The family tree looks like this:

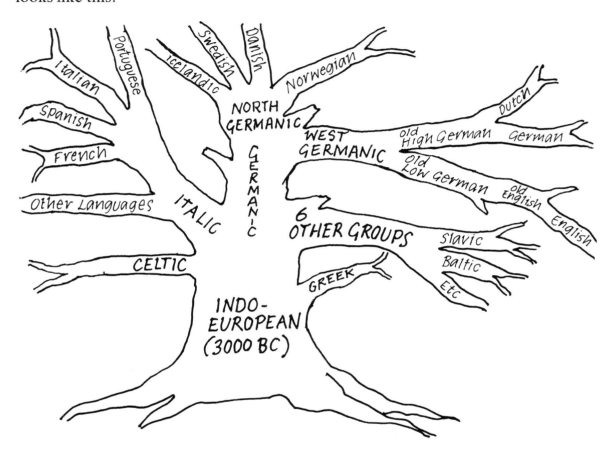

There are altogether about twenty important families of languages like this one, but the others are all a bit smaller.

You can see some remarkable family likenesses between the modern spoken languages of the Indo-European family. Look at these, for example:

(a) English: fish
    German: Fisch
    Dutch: fiche
    Danish: fisk
    Italian: pesce
    French: pêche
    Spanish: pez
    Welsh: pysgod

(b) English: mother
    Gaelic: máthair
    German: Mutter
    Dutch: moeder
    Swedish: moder
    Spanish: madre
    Italian: madre
    Welsh: mam

Rumanian: mamă

Hindi: mata (माता)

Bengali: mata (মা)

(c)

English: three	Gaelic: trí	Greek: treis (τρεῖς)
Spanish: tres	Czech: tři	Hindi: tee n (तीन)
Portuguese: três	Rumanian: trei	
Italian: tre	French: trois	Russian: tre (ТРИ)
Swedish: tre	German: drei	
Albanian: tre, tri	Dutch: drie	Bengali: tee n (তিন)
Welsh: tri		

And look at the Hindi word 'ta ma tar' (टमाटर)
Does it remind you of an English word? To-ma-to?

There are some particularly strong family likenesses between French and English. The French gave the English a lot of new words (some of which you will see in Activity 5) when William the Conqueror brought his army over from France to invade England in 1066, more than 900 years ago. The French army won the famous Battle of Hastings, and after the battle a lot of the French soldiers stayed in England. They used their language to govern the country and the people they had conquered. So the English had to learn to understand and also to use new French words. The new words stayed in the English language and we still use some of them today, even if they have changed a little since 1066.

Activity 5

Here are some French words which have been 'borrowed' by English, and changed a bit. Find out what these words are now in English. You could even make a good guess at some of them.

| théâtre | duc |
| soldat | chaise |

officier	cheminée
général	palais
mouton	bœuf

If you say these words out loud, even if you are not making the sounds quite as a French person would, you can *hear* the family likeness between French and English, as well as seeing it. Try it out.

English has also 'borrowed' and changed a lot of German words. Here are a few of them. Try to find out what they are. Saying them out loud again might help.

Apfel	Leder
Bier	Ding
Mann	Brot
Nummer	Schokolade
Markt	Papier

You can see and hear how close these German words are to the English ones, though of course not all German words are as nearly the same as these are. Many of their words sound (and look) nothing like our words at all.

14

Where did English come from?

Most of the language that we now speak and call 'English' has actually been 'borrowed' at one time or another from other countries. It is an imported language. It was first spoken by invaders coming over from what is now called Holland and North Germany. These were the Saxons, the Jutes, and the Angles (who, of course, spoke Engl-ish). The English language probably then sounded more like modern German. It was mainly spoken and only sometimes written down, using a different alphabet to the one we use now. They called it the Runic Alphabet. But a lot of words from this Old English language have grown up and changed into the English of today. Look at these for example:

camb   comb

docga   dog

cnif   knife

hors   horse

glaes   glass

Old English has left some other important bits behind which we still use today. They called their gods Tiw, Woden, Thor, and Frigg. From the names of these gods we get:

Tuesday	Tiw's day
Wednesday	Woden's day
Thursday	Thor's day
Friday	Frigg's day

English has also 'borrowed' words straight from Greek and Latin, and from other parts of the world, if ever a new word was needed.

Activity 6

Try to find out where these words have come from for us to use in our language. Give either the name of the language or of the country, or both if you can. You may find an atlas is useful for this.

1 wigwam, tomahawk, mocassin
2 vodka, tundra, sputnik
3 spaghetti, umbrella, bandit, volcano
4 poodle, dachshund, lager, blitzkrieg
5 telephone, telescope, telegram
6 canyon, rodeo, vanilla, bonanza
7 karate, kimono, samurai, hara-kiri
8 sofa, giraffe, sherbet, magazine

15

Family differences

So you can see that instead of thinking that English ways of speaking and writing have been made up by English people, we have to admit that they have in fact travelled to us from all over the world through hundreds of years of history. Our language is part of a huge family of languages, in which French and German are our first cousins.

All languages are useful for everyday jobs like making jokes, asking questions, talking on television or radio, reading the newspaper, and so on. The list of ways in which languages are used is endless.

Each one of the thousands of languages of the world does these jobs in a slightly different way. Its words are different from other languages and the way words are put together in sentences is a little different, and the things people talk about may be different too. You can think of the different languages as being built like different buildings, of different sizes, shapes, and colours, and for slightly different purposes. In the next few lessons we will think about some of the ways in which languages are built.

Things to discover

1 Russian, German, French, Spanish, and Italian are all languages which are used in Europe. On a map of Europe, using an atlas to help you, find the countries where these languages are used and write in the word for 'three' on your map, over the right country (see page 14). Put in any other words for 'three' whose language and country you can find also. You will see that most parts of Europe are linked in this way.

2 Here are the names of some countries you may have heard of: find out the names of their languages. Some of them have more than one!

Holland, Argentina, Switzerland, Canada, Israel

If you don't know where these countries are, find them on a map of the world.

3 Without looking back at what you have read in this unit, write down the answers to these questions:
(a) About how many languages are there in the world?
(b) Name two parts of the 'mouth-machine' that do *not* move when you speak, and two parts that *do* move.
(c) What language-family does English belong to? And what family does French belong to?
(d) What big reason is there in history for a strong likeness between some words in French and English?

4 If you have a collection of stamps from other countries, bring them to school so that you can all look at the different kinds of alphabet that some other countries use. Try to find out (a) what the names of these countries are and (b) the name of the language written on their stamps.

THE MATERIALS FOR THE JOB

Language-walls

If you have ever looked closely at a brick wall you will have noticed that each brick in it is a slightly different colour to the ones near it, and maybe a little bigger or smaller, maybe sticking out a little more than the bricks next to it, and so on. Words are rather like bricks in that way. Each word is different to the ones near it, and each one has a different 'message' in it. The whole message of a sentence is made up of all the words in it, just like the wall is made up of all the bricks in it. And in just the same way as one colour of brick may come up more than once in the wall, so one word, or one piece of a word, may come up again and again in a sentence. Each time a *piece* of a word is used it seems to have more or less the *same meaning*, the *same effect* on the whole word in which it is used.

Activity 1

Look at these things which you see written or hear said every day. They can all be broken down into 'bricks'.

First of all, where would you see or hear these words?

17

Now look at the first example, 'Good afternoon!' There are two words, but these two words are actually made up of *three* bricks. The word 'good' is one brick, but the word 'afternoon' is made up of two bricks, 'after' and 'noon'. Remember that in English one word can be made up of more than one brick.

The three pieces of 'Good afternoon!' can be found in other language 'walls' (other sentences or other words):

1 Good: Good enough, **good**-looking, **good**bye, thank **good**ness!
2 After: After all, **after** dinner, **after**wards, **after**thought.
3 Noon: At noon, **noon**day sun, high **noon**.

Now look at 'No parking'. This is also made up of three bricks. Here are the pieces of 'No parking' that can be found in other groups of words:

1 No: Nobody, **no** man's land, **no**thing, **no** entry.
2 Park: Car park, **park** gates, **park**ing-meter, **park**ing-ticket.
3 -ing: walk**ing**, laugh**ing**, swimm**ing**, eat**ing**, bark**ing**.

Now, break up the other blocks of words given above and try to think of other short sentences (or other words) in which the same pieces can be used again with the same sort of meaning in them.

Finding the meanings-pieces

So how small can these 'meanings-pieces' of words be? The smallest pieces may be made up of just one letter, and the bigger pieces may be whole words that you can recognize. The important thing is that you can *hear* them as separate pieces when the words are said out loud. If you read the words in this English language-wall out loud, you will notice how some pieces are used again and again, and you can *hear* them again and again as you read. The other important thing about pieces of words is that they can be used more than once, with the same sort of *meaning* each time.

The	great	-est	foot	ball	-er	of	all
is	certain	-ly	Pélé.	He	is	a	South
America	-n.	He	kick	-s	and	control	-s
the	ball	more	clever	-ly	than	other	
play	-er	-s.	No	Russia	-n	-s	or	Austria
-n	-s	are	real	-ly	in	his	class.

You can see that the '-s', the '-er', and the '-ly' come up more than once in this wall, and could be used in lots of other words in other walls.

Activity 2

Now look at this wall of words and find pieces of the words which are used *in more than one brick* in it. Write down a list of these pieces:

Penguin	-s	and	elephant	-s	like	go	-ing	in

-to	the	water	but	elephant	-s	can	not	swim

because	their	trunk	-s	are	too	long	and	get

in	the	way	of	their	arm	-s	when	they

are	try	-ing	to	do	front	crawl.	Maybe	if

they	went	in	with	-out	their	trunk	-s	on	they

'd	go	a	bit	fast	-er	and	swim	for	a	lot

long	-er	than	their	friend	-s	the	penguin	- s

1 Now build one small language-wall for each different piece of this big wall that you have in your list. Remember that some of these bricks may be whole words already and some are just bits of words. You should have found more than twelve pieces for your list.

2 Find *any* other brick in the wall, and you will see that you could have used it in a completely different wall if you had wanted to. Give any one bit of the wall to a friend, and ask him or her to use it in making a new language-wall.

Activity 3

Here are some groups of English words in which at least one of the pieces is used in more than one word in the group. You will have seen that words can actually be broken into smaller pieces than you may have thought. Find the pieces which are used more than once in each group.

Example: repeatedly, remotely, reportedly, excitedly
= **re-** (3 times), **-ed** (3 times), **-ly** (4 times)

1 remind, remember, resale, readjust
2 disturb, disbelieve, disgrace, believer, builder
3 undeveloped, unlikely, untied, nearly
4 repay, payment, argument, payable, reliable
5 painless, penniless, lesser, fewer, older
6 blackberry, strawberry, raspberry, blackest, ripest

The pieces of these words that you will have been able to find may not be whole words themselves, but you can probably think of other words in which the same pieces are used again.

It's not only English words that are made of pieces like this, pieces that can be used again and again in making different words. German and French and Spanish are three other languages in Europe that work in the same sort of way, although not all languages in the world do. Look at these groups of French words and try to find the pieces that are used more than once in them.

1 étrange, étrangement, étranger, étrangeté

2 boulangère, ménagère, fermière, bouchère

3 princesse, faiblesse, noblesse, vitesse, largesse

4 défaire, défendre, déborder, décapiter, détacher

5 remettre, rechercher, recommencer, recommander

6 indigestion, inférieur, indicible, incapable

Putting the pieces together

Germans tend to stick whole words together, as well as pieces of words, to make up a new word with another meaning. Here are a few 'cemented' pieces of German words, and what they mean when they are stuck together.

Abend = evening
Essen = meal, food
Abendessen = supper

Zahn = tooth
Arzt = doctor
Zahnarzt = dentist

Kugel = ball
Spritze = squirter
Kugelspritze = machine-gun

Kühl = cool
Schrank = cupboard
Kühlschrank = fridge

Now look at this long German word. It is a joke-word which means 'lollipop'. What it really means is 'children's novelty with a wooden handle'. You can see that it is really made up of lots of different pieces stuck together. Try saying it. It's quite a mouthful for a lollipop, isn't it? The whole word:

Kinderattraktionmithölzernehandangriff
(kin-der-a-trak-tsi-ohn-mit-hol-tser-ně-hant-an-grif)

The pieces:
Kind + er + attraktion + mit + hölz + ern + e + hand + an + griff

So you see how a long word can be made of several different pieces!

 Activity 4

Now look at what these bits of words in German mean, and try to work out what they might mean when they are cemented together.

1 Fuss = foot
Ball = ball
Fussball = ?

2 Kranken = sick people
Schwester = sister
Krankenschwester = ?

3 Kartoffel = potato
Suppe = soup
Kartoffelsuppe = ?

4 fünf = five
und = and
zwanzig = twenty
fünfundzwanzig = ?

5 Zahn = tooth
Bürste = brush
Zahnbürste = ?

6 Butter = butter
Brot = bread
Butterbrot = ?

7 früh = early
Stück = bit (of food)
Frühstück = ?

8 fern = far away, long-distance
Sprecher = speaker
Fernsprecher = ?

Masculine and feminine

In many European languages, such as Spanish, French, and Italian, all the nouns – the words for people and things – are divided into two groups, 'masculine' words and 'feminine' words. Every person and every thing is either masculine or feminine in *gender*.

How can we tell which words are masculine and which are feminine? Well, sometimes there are meanings-pieces in the words which tell us. Let's look at Spanish, for example. Here are some of the members of the Spanish family, the men on the left, the women on the right. Can you find the *piece* of each word which tells you the difference between the men and the women?

primo (boy cousin)   **prima** (girl cousin)

abuelo (grandad)   **abuela** (grandma)

hijo (son)   **hija** (daughter)
hermano (brother)   **hermana** (sister)

tío (uncle)   **tía** (aunt)

You will have seen that some of these Spanish words end with an '-o' and some of them end with an '-a'. It is the '-o' or the '-a' on the end of the words which usually tells you about the gender of the word. In Spanish, words for people or things which end in '-o' are 'masculine' in gender, and words for people or things which end in '-a' are 'feminine' in gender.

So we know that 'abuel**o**' is masculine and 'abuel**a**' is feminine, 'prim**o**' is masculine and 'prim**a**' is feminine, and so on.

Now look at these words in Spanish, and decide whether they are masculine or feminine in gender. You will find out in the same way as you did with the words for the members of the Spanish family.

alumno	**alumna**
(boy pupil)	(girl pupil)
moza	**mozo**
(waitress)	(waiter)
novio	**novia**
(boyfriend)	(girlfriend)
libro	**libra**
(book)	(pound)
pera	**perro**
(pear)	(dog)
helado	**naranja**
(ice cream)	(orange)
manzana	**vino**
(apple)	(wine)

You can see from these words that even words for things like books or fruit have a gender – they are either masculine or feminine. This is a useful way of remembering some words in Spanish.

It's not always that easy!

But what about words in Spanish, like the word **madre** (which means 'mother'), or **padre** (which means 'father')? These words do not end in '-o' or '-a', so how do we know if they are in the masculine class or in the feminine class? Luckily for us the Spanish give us another clue. They cement an extra little brick in front of their words for people or things. They say '**un** padre', '**un** abuelo', '**un** libro'. When we see or hear the word '**un**' (you say this word 'oon' to rhyme with 'spoon') we know that the person-or-thing word near it is masculine. Words which are feminine have the extra little brick '**una**' (you say this 'oo-nă') in front of them, even if they do not end in '-a'. So the Spanish say, '**una** madre', '**una** tía', '**una** manzana', and we know that these words are feminine.

The French do the same thing. They cement in an extra little brick to show which gender class a word is in. If you see or hear the word '**un**' (you say this 'ŭ(n)') in front of a French person-or-thing word, then you know it is in the masculine gender class. But if you hear or see '**une**' ('een') in front of a word, you know it is in the feminine gender class.

The gender of a word can make all the difference to the way a whole language-wall is built in languages like Spanish and French. If you make a mistake with the gender, the whole language-wall will be wrongly built. Here are two French language-walls. They have different numbers of bricks in them. Some extra bricks are needed to make the feminine wall properly which are not needed to make the masculine wall properly. If you left out these extra feminine bricks you might end up saying the wrong thing, building the wrong sort of wall completely.

Masculine wall (8 bricks)

| Un | ancien | ami | est | venu | me | visit | -er |

(An old friend – a *man* – came to visit me)

Feminine wall (12 bricks)

| Un | -e | ancien | -ne | ami | -e | est | venu | -e | me | visit | -er |

(An old friend – a *woman* – came to visit me)

The first clue you have for the difference in the *meaning* of the two sentences is in the extra bricks you hear or see which make 'un**e** ami**e**' belong to the feminine gender class – and this changes the number of bricks used in the whole wall.

So when you are learning a language which divides its nouns into masculine words and feminine words, it is very important to learn the gender of each new noun you learn. If you are learning German, you will find that nouns are divided into *three* gender classes. The extra class is called the 'neuter' class. So in German there are masculine words, feminine words, and neuter words!

Plurals

It is most important to remember that not all languages cement the pieces of their words together into sentences in the same way as, say, we do in English, or as we have seen the Spanish or Germans do in their languages. Not all languages work in the same way.

In English, for example, if we want to make sure that we are talking about *more than one* thing, we usually just add an '-s' or '-es' to the end of the word when we write it down. We 'put it into *the plural*'. But have you ever thought of the different noises that '-s' will make when you *say* the word with your mouth-machine, instead of writing it? Read these words out loud, and you will hear.

(cat + s)	cats
(book + s)	books
(plate + s)	plates
(cup + s)	cups
(shirt + s)	shirts
(sock + s)	socks

This 's' makes the hissing sound 'sssss' at the end of the word. It is one of the *plural* sounds of English. Think of some more words with this hissing plural sound.

(dog + s)	dogs
(pen + s)	pens
(chair + s)	chairs
(shoe + s)	shoes
(tie + s)	ties
(jumper + s)	jumpers

This 's' makes the buzzing sound 'zzzzz' at the end of the word. This is

23

the second of the *plural* sounds in English. Try to think of some more 'buzzing' plurals.

(house + s)	houses
(face + s)	faces
(nose + s)	noses
(horse + s)	horses
(rose + s)	roses
(moose + s)	mooses

Here you will hear a 'siz' or 'ziz' sound at the end of the word. This is another separate *plural* sound used in English. Think of a few more words with this plural sound at the end – they are usually for words with a 'sss' or 'zzz' sound at the end already.

Of course there are other ways in English that we can show that we are talking about *more than one* of something, without making any of the three 's' sounds at the end. What about this, for example:

– I saw a *woman* at the fair, selling balloons.

– Fred said there were lots of *women* there.

The two words 'woman' and 'women' *sound* quite different, even if they look almost the same. More than just one of the sounds has changed in the word to show that you mean *more than one* – if the 'woo' sound changes to the 'wi' sound in the first piece of the word, how does the second piece change its sound? You are, in fact, using your mouth-machine in a slightly different way to say each of these words.

Activity 6

What are the *plurals* of these words in English? Write them down first to make sure of your spelling, and then say them both out loud in pairs ('singular' column words first, then 'plural' column words) to hear what the difference in the noises you make is. Try to say *why* and *how* the words sound different – what are you doing differently with your mouth-machine and its voice-box part?

Singular	Plural
(only one)	(more than one)
one knife	five ......
one child	four ......
the bad hoof	its three good ......
(of the horse)	
one wife	six ......
an ox	two ......
a small white mouse	twenty white ......
a white sheep	three black ......
a small goldfish	two big ......
an angry goose	five angry ......

In Spanish, where you can also just add an '-s' or '-es' to the end of a word to make it plural, there are only two noises that the extra '-s' or '-es' can make. These are the hissing 'ssss' and the 'ess' sound (like saying 'yes' without the 'y'). So now how do you think you would *write* the plurals of these words?

(a) **Hissing 's'**

1 chico   7 ......

1 casa   3 ......

1 mesa   5 ......

1 sombrero   9 ......

(b) **'ess'** (rhymes with 'yes')
(Here you will have to add an '-es' to the end
of the words to make them plural.)

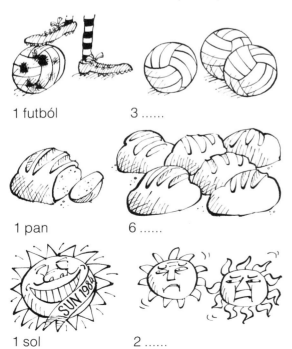

1 futból   3 ......

1 pan   6 ......

1 sol   2 ......

1 revolver   2 ......

More plurals

In some kinds of English, such as West
Indian English, people make the plural
in a different way when they mean
'more than one'. They don't only add
an '-s' brick but they also add a whole
extra brick: 'them'. You might hear a
West Indian say this:

   . . . the books them
   ('. . . de books dem')

when he is talking about more than one
book.

In some languages people don't bother
to add anything, not even an '-s', to
show whether something is in the
singular or plural – there is no extra
sound to show that they mean 'more
than one'! Malay, the language of
Malaysia, is one language like this.

'Pensil' in Malay could mean 'one
pencil' or 'several pencils' – they've
borrowed their word for 'pencil' from
English. Or 'anjing' could be

either   or

There is no '-s' on the end of the *plural*
word 'anjing' to make it sound any
different from the *singular* word
'anjing', so you just have to guess
which it is!

In Hindi, German, Russian, or French, different bricks are added to the end of some words to show that they mean *more than one*. Just as we put an '-s' on the end of words to show this in English, Indians who speak Hindi may put '-yem' $\left(\begin{smallmatrix} \psi \\ \overline{S} \end{smallmatrix}\right)$ or '-yam' or '-hem'

onto the end of the word. For example, 'mata' means 'mother', but 'matayem' means 'mothers'.

Each brick that you use to build up words or bigger pieces of language is made in a slightly different way. It has a slightly different colour or shape – it has its own special *meaning*. And each language makes up its words or word-walls in slightly different ways: as we've seen, not all languages make the same noises to mean 'more than one', do they? Spanish has two different sorts of noises for 's', and English uses three!

Things to discover

1 Find out as many English words as you can which end in either '-ology' (like biology) or '-ography' (like geography) or '-ish' (like greenish or smallish etc.). When you've made a list of words for each of the three endings, try to decide what *meaning* the ending seems to give the words.

2 Look in the front of a good English dictionary where it gives a list of *abbreviations*.

Find out what these letters are short for:

fem., zool., v., F., sing., pl., masc., O.E., sent., wd., Arab., Sp.

Abbreviations are another way in which *pieces* of words can sometimes give you a clue as to what the whole meaning of a word is.

3 Here are two adverts from a paper. You can just about understand them, even though a lot of the letters have been left out. What do they say?

> FOR SALE Modn hse on gd strt nr shops. Big gdn. Pkg space. 3 bdrms, bathrm, kit., lnge, oil cntl htg. £30,000 o.n.o.

> 1979 Rcd plyr and rdio with spkrs in v. gd cndtn. £40 o.n.o.

4 Often people use only the first letters of long names, what are called 'initials', instead of saying the whole name. 'B.B.C.' stands for British Broadcasting Corporation, and 'G.P.O.' is used instead of General Post Office. This is another way in which only bits of words are used, rather like in the dictionary abbreviations.

(a) What are the initials of your own name, and of the members of your family?

(b) What do the initials below stand for?

A.A., R.A.F., F.A., B.R., H.M., G.B., I.R.A., K.K.K., U.S.S.R.

5 Try to say whether these words end with a *hissing plural* or a *buzzing plural* or a *'siz'/'ziz' plural*. Say them out loud and listen to the sounds you make.

(a) fish fingers   (f) jams
(b) chips   (g) sweets
(c) peas   (h) choc-ices
(d) crisps   (i) coffees
(e) cakes   (j) milk-shakes

26

BUILDING WITH THE MATERIALS

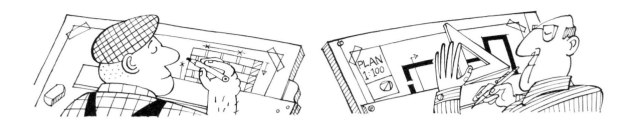

Making plans

Before people say anything to each other they first make at least two
different sorts of plans. First they think of what they want to say and what
they *mean*. They choose the right sort of word-bricks to make their
meanings as clear as possible. This sort of plan is the **meaning plan**. The
second sort of plan fixes the order in which the word-bricks should be
spoken so that the meaning is quite clear. This second sort of plan is the
speaking plan, and it is this type of plan which we will think about here.
Both these plans take less than a second or two to make and use in your
own language. You can answer a question in an instant, for example,
getting the right meaning and using the right plan quite naturally, without
even thinking about it.

When a house is being built, two sorts of plans are made as well. First
there are the drawing-plans made by the architect in his office: he plans
the main shape and size of the house, and of the rooms in it. That is like
the meaning plan. Then there is the builder's plan, made by the builder
and bricklayers and carpenters on the building site. These plans fix the
actual materials to be used and the order in which they will be used so that
the building is properly made. These are like the speaking plans. The two
sorts of plans for language (and for houses) go together: you cannot build
a sentence (or a house) properly without following them both carefully.

The thing to remember is that not all languages have the same speaking
plans as English does. Each different language builds slightly different
kinds of language-buildings by using its *own* speaking plans. When you
learn these new languages, part of the job is to learn to use new speaking
plans as quickly and as exactly as you use English speaking plans. That
takes practice, of course. Don't forget, you've been using and practising
English speaking plans ever since you were about two years old, when you
first started to speak, so you've had quite a long time to learn to use them
well!

27

If these speaking plans are so natural to us, and if we use them without having to think too much about them, how do we even know they are there?

Here are some English sentences that have been built *without* following the speaking plans properly. The meaning plan is there, and the word-bricks have been chosen properly, but that's all. There is no speaking plan and so the sentences are nonsense. Build a proper speaking plan into the word-bricks by putting the words in each sentence in the 'right order'.

1 Queen the save God!
2 Time a upon once, . . .
3 Four two make two and.
4 I comic my reading am.
5 Look like you hot dog a!
6 Salt could pass the please you?
7 Is the I Elvis greatest think.
8 Not are always horrible teachers.
9 Hot the Sahara is very desert.
10 Small in Marmite comes jars brown.

Another way of seeing that speaking plans *are* there even if we don't always know it is to cut an ordinary sentence up into 'bricks', like this:

1. Fred 2. is 3. very 4. thick

If you change round the order of the bricks, either the sentence turns into nonsense because the speaking plan has been taken away, like this:

3. Very 2. is 4. thick 1. Fred

Or else you can change the bricks round to fit slightly different speaking plans, like for asking a question:

2. Is 1. Fred 3. very 4. thick ?

In other words, plans numbers 1 2 3 4 and 2 1 3 4 (for questions) are both good plans in English, and each one is built a little differently even though the main meaning

and the word-bricks stay the same. But plan number 3 2 4 1 is nonsense, and you wouldn't use it at all: it is not an English speaking plan.

Here is plan number 1 2 3 4 again, and all sorts of different bricks that you could use in the same order, using the same speaking plan, but just changing the meaning by changing the bricks you use each time. Use the different bricks to build as many different sentences as you can, but remember to use speaking plan number 1 2 3 4 all the time.

The plan:

1. Fred 2. is 3. very 4. thick

The bricks you can use:

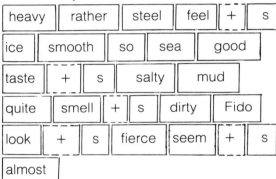

You will find that each of the new bricks will only fit into one box of the 1 2 3 4 plan. If you try to put the wrong brick into the wrong box, you will not be following the speaking plan properly and your language-wall will not do its job properly either. That is how important speaking plans are in sentences.

You can also see that you have to put two bricks – one main brick with one extra 's' brick stuck on – into box number 2 of the speaking plan. If you forgot the extra 's' brick in this box of the plan, your language wall would be wrong too, wouldn't it? Try leaving the 's' brick out, and you will see.

Changing the plan

Sometimes in English, and in other languages too, question-walls can just be made by using the same bricks a different way round.

1. | They | 2. | are | 3. | always |
4. | naughty |

can be made into a question-wall, using the same bricks.

2. | Are | 1. | they | 3. | always |
4. | naughty | ?

But sometimes in English and in other languages an extra brick or two may have to be added to make a proper, strong question-wall.

These bricks cannot be made into a question in English:

| You | | come | | here | | often |

We cannot just change them into

| Come | | you | | here | | often | ?

We must add an extra brick at the beginning of the wall to make it into a proper question:

| Do | | you | | come | | here | | often | ?

And we can even add another brick at the beginning to make a different question-wall:

| Why | | do | | you | | come | | here |
| often | ?

Remember, if we did not use slightly different speaking plans, which might need more or less bricks, to make questions and answers, nobody would ever be sure if we were asking a question or answering it!

And in just the same way we have to use different plans and different numbers of bricks when we want to give someone else an order, or say 'no' to them about something instead of 'yes', or change our meaning in other different little ways as we speak.

| Activity 3 | 🖎

Here are some question-walls which have been built by using the plans and the right number of bricks for making questions. Knock down each question wall and then use some or all of the *same* bricks to make good answers. Write the answer-walls down, and then count how many bricks from each question-wall you did *not* need to use to build your answer-wall.

1 | Do | | they | | like | | toast | | and | | jam | ?

2 | Is | | that | | big | | boy | | a | | bully | ?

3 | Is | | this | | little | | girl | | clever | ?

4 | Is | | my | | yorbo | | jitty | ?

5 | Do | | sploggs | | krate | | bombles | | drap |
| gurble | ?

You can see that sometimes you have one brick left over from the question-wall, and sometimes you have used up all the bricks in your answer-wall. The plans for the two sorts of wall are different. You can see too that in the last two question-walls a speaking plan is still there, even if the word-bricks don't really mean anything. You can still make nonsense answers to the nonsense questions. You still use plans. That just shows you what an important part speaking plans play in whatever you say.

Everyone needs speaking plans

Now we know that speaking plans are an important part of every English language-building that we all make every day. Without these plans, what we say would be nonsense.

French would be nonsense too if the French people didn't follow the rules and speaking plans of French. Germans have to follow their speaking plans properly too, and so do the Spanish, the Russians, the Chinese and so on. None of us – French, Chinese, English, or German – have to think much about the plans we follow to build sentences in our own languages. The right plans are just there in our heads, as if by magic. Of course we *can*, if we want, find out what the plans are and how they work, but we don't really *have* to know.

When you learn to speak another, new language, you try to learn to use a new set of speaking plans without having to stop and think about them. It will be important to learn to use the new word-bricks and new plans to make new language-buildings quickly and properly. Using the old, English plans that you have been using ever since you were two years old just won't work any more.

Activity 4

Here is Gaston. He is French. He is trying to say a few things in English, but he is still using French speaking plans. If you try saying some of the things he has said, out loud, you will *hear* how funny his English sounds. That is because he has forgotten to use English speaking plans. Try to give him the proper English plans, so that his sentences sound 'right'. You may have to change one or two of the word-bricks too.

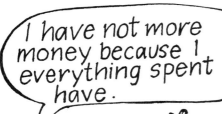

And here is Gustav. He is German, and he is still trying to use his German speaking plans to build English sentences, but they don't work either, do they? So try to give him the right English speaking plans.

You must remember that *you* might sound just as funny to either Gaston or Gustav if you tried to use English speaking plans to build sentences in French or German. They might feel like laughing at the odd things *you* tried to say. So the thing to do is to learn to use the speaking plans of *their* languages properly. After all, you will want them to understand what you are trying to say.

Language-walls that stretch and shrink

Not all the sentences that you speak and write are exactly as long as each other, are they? Some are shorter and some are longer. Well, the speaking plans of languages can be stretched or shrunk sometimes to allow you to build shorter or longer language-walls too. It is like using a plan for a wall of a house, but building the wall a bit longer or a bit shorter than the plan says. This means that speaking plans can sometimes grow longer or shorter, *without turning into different plans*. They are the same plans, but just in a different size.

Here is a short 1 2 3 plan. Parts 1 and 3 of this plan have two bricks each but part 2 only needs one brick.

We can make part one about the poodle longer and longer, like this, still using the 1 2 3 plan:

			1.				2.		3.	
(a)	The	little	poodle				bit		the	gorilla
(b)	The	little	yellow	poodle			bit		the	gorilla
(c)	The	little	yellow	poodle						
	with	a	green	tie	and					
	an	orange	jacket	on			bit		the	gorilla

Part 1 (a) of the plan has three bricks in it, part 1 (b) has four bricks in it, and then part 1 (c) has thirteen bricks in it, but the kind of plan used to build the sentence is always 1 2 3. We could have added exactly the same extra bricks to part 3 of the plan, about the gorilla, only then it would have changed the meaning of the sentence so that the *gorilla* and not the *poodle* would have been 'little, yellow, with a green tie and an orange jacket on'. The speaking plan would *still* have been in the 1 2 3 order.

Activity 5

Plan-stretching: Try stretching a few of the plans given to you here, but make sure that you do not change the speaking plan order. If you do change the order of the sections of any of these speaking plans you will be turning it into a completely new plan, and that won't count. Use some of the extra bricks given to you for making the language-walls longer, one or two bricks at a time.

Example:

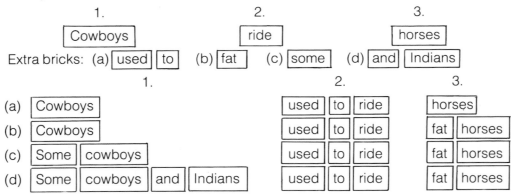

	1.	2.	3.
Cowboys	ride	horses

Extra bricks: (a) used to (b) fat (c) some (d) and Indians

		1.			2.			3.	
(a)	Cowboys				used	to	ride	horses	
(b)	Cowboys				used	to	ride	fat	horses
(c)	Some	cowboys			used	to	ride	fat	horses
(d)	Some	cowboys	and	Indians	used	to	ride	fat	horses

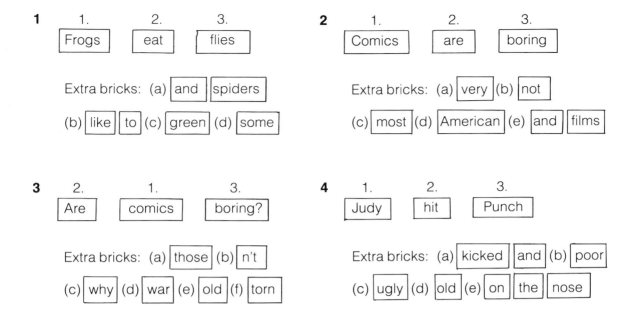

1
1. Frogs
2. eat
3. flies

Extra bricks: (a) and | spiders
(b) like | to (c) green (d) some

2
1. Comics
2. are
3. boring

Extra bricks: (a) very (b) not
(c) most (d) American (e) and | films

3
2. Are
1. comics
3. boring?

Extra bricks: (a) those (b) n't
(c) why (d) war (e) old (f) torn

4
1. Judy
2. hit
3. Punch

Extra bricks: (a) kicked | and (b) poor
(c) ugly (d) old (e) on | the | nose

By adding one or two of the extra bricks at a time and stretching one section of the plan each time, the whole sentence you will have built will have grown longer and its meaning will have grown too. But all the time the same number of sections for the speaking plan will have been there, even if the *inside* of each section has grown more and more complicated. So you see that even long and complicated language-walls can be built with quite easy speaking plans.

Activity 6

The same sort of thing can happen in languages like French or German or Spanish too. Here is a French language-wall that grows and grows each time it is written down. Find the new bricks that have been added to this French language-wall each time, and copy them down on paper.

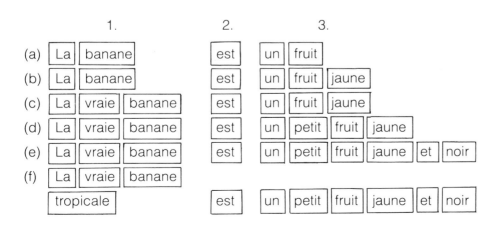

1. 2. 3.

(a) La | banane   est | un | fruit
(b) La | banane   est | un | fruit | jaune
(c) La | vraie | banane   est | un | fruit | jaune
(d) La | vraie | banane   est | un | petit | fruit | jaune
(e) La | vraie | banane   est | un | petit | fruit | jaune | et | noir
(f) La | vraie | banane
tropicale   est | un | petit | fruit | jaune | et | noir

Which means . . . 'The real tropical banana is a small yellow and black fruit.'

And here is a German language-wall which shrinks and shrinks, because a few bricks are taken away from one section of its plan each time until it can get no smaller. And yet the shape of the speaking plan stays just the same. Find the missing bricks each time and write them down.

1.

(a) | Die | alte | Tomate | mit | dem |
roten | Gesicht | und | dem |
grünen | Haar |

(b) | Die | alte | Tomate | mit | dem |
roten | Gesicht |

(c) | Die | alte | Tomate | mit | dem |
roten | Gesicht |

(d) | Die | alte | Tomate |

(e) | Die | alte | Tomate |

(f) | Die | alte | Tomate |

(g) | Die | Tomate |

2.

(a) liebte | sehr

(b) liebte | sehr

(c) liebte

(d) liebte

(e) liebte

(f) liebte

(g) liebte

3.

(a) die | junge | und
schöne | Runkelrübe

(b) die | junge | und
schöne | Runkelrübe

(c) die | junge | und
schöne | Runkelrübe

(d) die | junge | und
schöne | Runkelrübe

(e) die | junge | Runkelrübe

(f) die | Runkelrübe

(g) die | Runkelrübe

And this is what it all means:

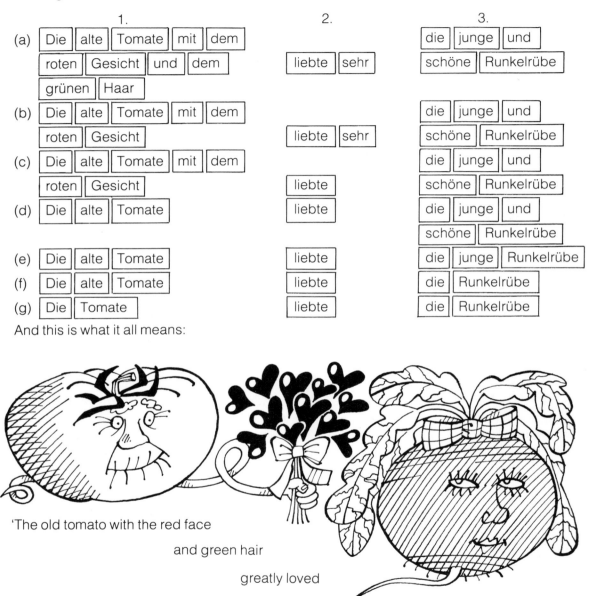

'The old tomato with the red face

and green hair

greatly loved

the young, beautiful beetroot.'

So now you can see how other languages like French or German have speaking plans just as we have them in our English language-walls. Just the same as in English too, their plans can be stretched or shrunk without changing the order of the plan, or else the order can be turned round a bit so that different, new speaking plans are being used. Their speaking plans are just as invisible as ours are, but just as important if you are going to be able to say exactly what you *mean*.

1 When you learn a new language, you may come across these words now and then:

interrogative
negative
imperative

Use a good dictionary or encyclopaedia to help you find out what these words mean – what would be other, more ordinary words for the same ideas? They are all names for different sorts of sentence, built by using slightly different kinds of speaking plans.

2 Now here are some short English sentences which are either *interrogative* or *negative* or *imperative*. Say which one of the three kinds you think each sentence is:

(a) Give us a hand!
(b) How are you?
(c) What do you mean?
(d) I'm not tired.
(e) Get out, quick!
(f) No, he can't swim.
(g) Wait here!
(h) When?
(i) He never drinks water.
(j) Are you coming?

3 A *sentence* is a group of words, made with *one* speaking plan, which tells us about one whole idea or thought. This is a sentence, made with a short 1 2 3 speaking plan:

1.   2.   3.

| Fred | is | | a   good   bloke |

Now try to find the complete 1 2 3 speaking-plans, the whole sentences, in all these words. Write down the sentences one underneath the other as you find them. There are nine sentences to find.

Fred	is	a	good	bloke	he
likes	football		he	watches	
matches	he	supports	Liverpool		
Liverpool	are	great	they	won	
the	cup	I	support	Liverpool	
they	are	my	favourite	team	
Fred	is	my	best	friend	

When people *speak* sentences, it may not be easy to tell where the sentences end. But when we *write* sentences it is easy to see the beginning and end of them. Why? What do we see there?

WORD-BRICKS — MEANING PLANS

Saying what you mean

We know that there are two sorts of plans that have to be made so that what we say *makes sense* and sounds as clear as possible. The **speaking plan** may make the words we actually say as clear as possible, but it is in fact the **meaning plan** which is there first, and which gives us the first ideas about what we are going to try and say. The meaning plans, you remember, are rather like the first plans made for a house by the architect in his office. He sits at his drawing-board and draws paper-plans for the *idea* of the house. It is the builder who then turns those ideas into bricks and cement, into rooms and doors and windows.

We know too that sentences can be built without any real meaning plan, without any real idea behind them, but still using an English speaking plan. Here is a sentence built like that;

1.
| Green | idea | s |

2.
| run | loud | ly |

The speaking plan is number 1–2, and the word-bricks are all perfectly ordinary English ones, but they don't fit together in any meaning plan, and so the sentence doesn't mean anything. It is nonsense. So you can see that both sorts of plans are very important to the meaning of the sentence, and that both sorts of plans must be properly used.

Where do meaning plans start from, then? Somewhere inside our heads ideas start out as pictures or feelings.

Before we can *say* what that picture or feeling is, we need to have a word for it that the other people around us will understand. Language is useful for talking to other people, not for talking to ourselves, so that we all have to use noises that other people will understand when we want to put our meanings into words.

Activity 1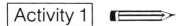

Look at these pictures and *without saying anything* to anyone else, write down the word in English that you think goes with each picture.

1

2

3

4

5

6

When you've written down the six words that you think go with the pictures, see what other people have written down for the same pictures. You will probably find that you all agree about words for the first two pictures, but maybe you don't agree about what words to use for the last few pictures. You see, you will have had different *ideas* about what those things are, and then used different word-bricks to *say* what you think they are to other people. You may think you have 'seen' quite different things in the last two pictures and so had to use different words to say what they were.

If you had been speaking Spanish or Russian or Zulu, for example, you would have had exactly the same *idea* as you have just had when you saw those pictures, but you would have used Spanish or Russian or Zulu word-bricks to say what you thought they were to other people. The English word-bricks that you have just written down would not have *meant* anything at all to them. You would have had to use *their* noises which had the right meaning in *their* language. And that would have been the beginning of the meaning plan for what you were going to say.

37

Activity 2

There are some people who can't hear or speak as most people can. These people, the deaf or the dumb, have made up sign languages to say things to each other with, and they use their hands to make words which are *seen* and understood instead of being *heard* and understood. But even if they don't say what their ideas and meanings are by using their mouth-machines, they still mean the same things and have the same sort of ideas as we all do.

Look at these drawings of some of the signs that you would use to 'talk' with and to say what your ideas were if you were deaf or dumb. Try to use them silently to 'say' something to someone else. Just 'say' one idea at a time, and see if your idea can be understood and written down in English by the other person.

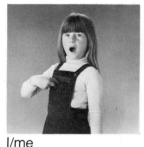
I/me

you

go

come

cinema

school

stupid

bored

hate

love

give

money

Here are some things you can say with these signs:

I am **going** to the **cinema**.
I am **going** to **school**.
Are **you bored**?
Give me some **money**.
I **hate school**.
I **love you**.
You are **stupid**.

And you can think of other things to say too.

In sign-language, just like in spoken language of any kind, an idea and a sign-word are put together in your mind before you start to fit them into a meaning plan and speaking plan of the right shape for the job. When you make sign-words, you still *mean* exactly the same thing as you would if you said the words out loud, and you still have the same idea in your head, even though you don't say anything.

38

Ideas and words

The signs you would make in sign-language are the word-bricks of that language. Word-bricks are the first step in any meaning plan. You start off with an idea and find a word that goes with that idea. Then you begin to put two or more ideas together in some sort of planned order, so that their meanings 'hang together'. Then you begin to put them into a proper speaking plan and find the right sort of noises to make with your mouth-machine so that you can actually *say* your ideas in the way you want other people to understand them. All of this takes only a split second to do in your own language, but it may take a bit longer in someone else's language, like in sign-language, for example.

In Cowboy and Indian films, the Indians usually speak in very simple sentences which have very simple meaning plans. They say only the most important words and they miss out a lot of the smaller 'cement' words from their language-walls. They speak like this (but real Indians don't!):

– Me Chief Sitting Bull. Who you?
– Me Great Thundercloud.
– What you want?
– Long time no rain. Paleface come. Buffalo leave plain. Children starve. No food. We hunt together?
– First we hunt Paleface. Commanche and Sioux great warrior. Together we send Paleface from land. Then Buffalo return. Then food.

We can all understand this sort of language quite well. Only the important word-bricks are used and these are put in the right order for the meaning of each word to help and fit together with the meaning of the other words. We could finish off these sentences by using an English speaking plan and building complete, proper English language-walls. But even at this stage in the building, the *meaning* is clearly there.

| Activity 3 | |

Now it is your turn to have an Indian 'pow-wow' with a friend. Do not use *any* extra words in what you say. Work out what the important word-bricks are in your sentences and use *only* them, so that only the real meaning plan is left. Here are the things you can talk about. Choose one 'pow-wow', work it out carefully with a friend, and practise it so that you could act it like a short play.

Start by saying: *Your names? Your tribes? Where you live?*

1 Some Stolen Horses: how many, what they **look like**, **where** you think they are, **who** may have **stolen** them, **what** you **want to do** about it.

2 The Railway Line being built: **who** is **building** it, **why** you **don't like** it, **what** you think the **railway will do**, **what** you want to do to **stop it**.

3 The Waggon Train: where it is **now**, **where** it is **going**, **what** you think it is **doing**, **who** is in the waggons, **how many soldiers** are with them, **why** and **how** you want to stop it.

4 The Cavalry Fort: who is building it, **where** it is, **why** you **don't like** it there, **how** you want to **attack** it, **how many warriors** will be needed, **how** you will get **guns**.

5 The Rattlesnakes: how many people have been **killed** by **snakes**, **why** you think the **gods** have sent the snakes, **how** you think you can work together to **beat the rattlesnakes** and **please the gods**.

You will only have used the word-bricks that you *really* had to use to make your meaning plan quite clear in the pow-wow that you built. You *could* have gone on from the simple meaning plan stage, to think of the whole, proper speaking plan and to build whole, proper English sentences. That is what you normally do in the things you say in English. The speaking plan turns your meaning plan into a strongly-built language-wall, of exactly the type that you want to make.

Mabel builds a language-wall

Here is Mabel thinking of the different ways in which she could turn her ideas first into word-bricks and then build those bricks into lots of different sorts of language-walls. Some of these language-walls may be orders or questions or requests or just telling someone something.

She is looking and . . .

This idea turns into a word-brick.

Next she thinks . . .

Which turns into another word-brick.

And what will she *do* with the bone?

The third idea also turns into a word-brick, like this:

GIVE

So she has three main word-bricks, three main pieces of meaning in her meaning plan.

DOG **GIVE** **BONE**

She changes them round and starts fitting these pieces into a *speaking plan* now.

GIVE **DOG** **BONE**

And now she can put these main bricks into different language-walls if she uses slightly different speaking plans, but they all come from the same three pieces of the *meaning* plan.

> Please **give** the **dog** that **bone**.

> Have you **given** the **dog** that **bone**?

> **Give** the **dog** a **bone**, will you?

> Just **give** the **dog** any **bone**, for Pete's sake.

In all these things that Mabel can say, you can see the three main meaning bricks. She could also have added some other bricks too, like horrible/huge/nasty, if she had wanted to add extra pieces of meaning to the main bricks.

> I'm not going to **give** that horrible **dog** my chicken **bone**.

> I told you not to **give** that nasty bull**dog** such a huge **bone**, didn't I?

Activity 4

Now it's your turn.

1 First of all, turn these ideas into word-bricks and write down just the main bricks that you will use, just like Mabel did. Write only *one* word for each idea bubble that you see.

(a)

(b)

(c)

41

(d)

(e)

2 Next, look at the word-bricks that you have thought of for each idea given in the bubbles, and think how many *other, different* word-bricks you could have used for that same idea, instead of just the one you did choose. You will find that the pictures could mean lots of different things, and you could have used all sorts of different word-bricks for them. But you just chose one word-brick, and that was the beginning of your meaning plan. Someone else may have chosen different word-bricks with slightly different meanings and would have ended up with different meaning plans. What words did your friends choose?

3 Next, think of one sentence (using a proper English speaking plan) into which the word-bricks you chose for each idea would fit easily and in which they would sound 'right'. When you do this, you will be turning the meaning plan into a speaking plan, ready to be spoken out loud. Write down the sentences you build.

4 Lastly, go back to your word-bricks for each idea from the pictures and make as many different commands or questions or ordinary sentences out of the *same* bricks as you can. Your main meaning plan will be the same in all of them, but you will have used a different speaking plan to make each new sentence, question, or command. Try to make at least three new sentences for each one.

If you hadn't used meaning plans or speaking plans for all these sentences you would have made up nonsense noises instead of good English language-walls.

Activity 5

Sometimes, in any language, you might say something, and other people might *hear* it as something different to what you mean. They think you mean something else, because the words you have used can mean two different things. When this happens, two different meaning plans have been built with the same word-bricks, and you think that the other person has 'got hold of the wrong end of the stick'. You have said what you mean, but they have taken your words in a different way. It can be very annoying.

Look hard at this picture and see if you can see two different things in it. Write down what you think they are.

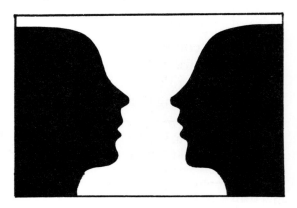

You will have seen two completely different things drawn with one set of lines.

Some words can be like that too: you can sometimes see two different meanings in one word. Look at these riddles. In one word in either the riddle or its answer there are two meanings, which gives each riddle two different meaning plans. Try to answer the riddles and then say what the word with two meanings is.

1 What runs but never walks?
2 What has two hands but no arms?
3 What has got teeth but cannot bite?
4 How do you make an egg roll?
5 Why do cows wear bells?
6 Who drives away all his best customers?
7 What sort of person is always fed up with other people?
8 What word if you say it right is wrong, but if you say it wrong is right?

Now, it is sometimes quite easy to guess what the meaning of a word in another language is too, even if you have never seen it before. In the riddles that you have (I hope) been able to answer, you were able to see the two *meanings* of one of the word-bricks, or guess the two different meaning plans that the sentence may have been built on. You would do the same sort of thing in working out what a foreign word was that you didn't know. You would see if you could understand what the meaning plan was by looking at all the other word-bricks in the sentence. Here are some sentences in which there is a foreign word instead of an

English one. Write down what you think that word means, after reading the whole sentence carefully to see how it fits into the whole meaning plan. Try to say what other word-bricks in each sentence you used as clues to the meaning of the foreign word.

1 He shook his golden mane and roared over the dead zebra. The **simba** had hunted well today and now he was hungry.

2 Sleeping in a tree not far away, the **chui** heard the roar. He stretched his spotted coat and sharpened his claws against the tree before he went off in search of an antelope for supper.

3 At the pool, the **tembo** was having a drink and spraying water with his trunk on to his huge back.

4 The splashing of the water made the little **samaki** jump out of the water. Their scales were silver in the sunshine of the afternoon.

5 And a big **tumbili** chattered and laughed at them, sitting up on a branch with a ripe orange in his hand, which he was about to eat. He had to grip tight with his tail, so as not to fall off the branch, because he was laughing so hard.

(All these foreign words come from a language called Swahili, which is spoken by people in East Africa.)

Saying the same thing . . . in different ways

Even when you change not just one, but *all* the word-bricks into another language, the *meaning* of what you are saying will stay the same. In other words, the meaning plan for your ideas will be the same, even though the sounds that you make with your mouth-machine and the speaking plan that you have used to put those sounds in the right order will be different to the English ones.

Here is an example of the way the idea (and the meaning plan) stays the same even if the sounds you would make do not stay the same. In English, when we see each other first thing in the morning we usually say 'Good morning'. But when people want to say the same sort of thing in other languages, these are the words they use:

An Italian:

(bwon **jor**-noh)

A Frenchman:

(bawn-**zhoor**)

A Greek:

(kal-ee-**mair**-ă)

A German:

(**goo**-těn **tahg**)

A Malay:

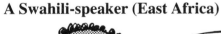

(slah-maht pă-**gee**)

A Spaniard:

(bway-noss **dee**-ass)

A Swahili-speaker (East Africa)

(**jam**-boh)

44

An American:

Hi

A Hindi speaker (India):

नमस्ते
Namaste

(năm-ăss-**tay**)

A Punjabi speaker (India):

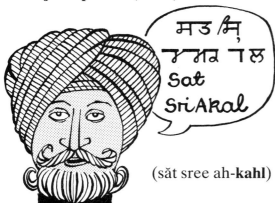

ਸਤ ਸ੍ਰੀ
ਅਕਾਲ
Sat
SriAkal

(săt sree ah-**kahl**)

We could find hundreds and hundreds of completely different ways in which people say the same idea to each other when they first see each other each morning – these are just a few of them, but you can see how different the word-bricks are even though the idea is the same.

Activity 7

Here are some sentences written in other people's languages. In these sentences there are one or two hidden words which you will be able to guess from the same English word if you look hard and listen hard. Your teacher will say the sentences out loud by following the pronunciation guide given. You should be able to *hear* the meaning plan of the sentence by hearing the hidden words and thinking about how they fit together. Find and write down what you think the *meaning plan* for each sentence is. You may not be able to guess exactly what the whole sentence would be in English – that is where the speaking plan would take over.

An example from Italian: Quello è un autobus inglese?
Pronunciation guide: (**kwel**-loh e oon **ow**-toh-buus een-**glay**-say)
Possible word-bricks: ? ? ? bus English
Proper meaning: Is that an English bus?

1 *Italian:*
Quella è una bottiglia di birra?
(**kwel**-lă e **oo**-nă bot-**ee**-lee-ă dee **bee**-ră)

2 *French:*
Oui, c'est une bouteille de bière.
(wee, set een boo-**tay** dĕ bee-**air**)

3 *German:*
Hier ist dein altes Buch.
(heer ist dyn **al**-tĕs boo*ch*) (*ch* as in 'loch')

4 *Spanish:*
Este diccionario no es mío.
(**es**-tay dik-thi-o-**nah**-ri-oh noh ess **mee**-oh)

5 *French:* Mon oncle est stupide.
(mon awnkl e stee-**peed**)

6 *German:*
Und mein Bruder ist dumm.
(oont myn **broo**-der ist duum)

Of course, you would be lucky if there were many word-bricks in a sentence in another language that you could guess that easily. But at least you should be able to see that you *can* find the meaning plan on which a whole sentence is built by looking for the most important word-bricks in it, and seeing how these bricks fit together.

Things to discover

1 The *idea* of each of these sentences (and the whole meaning plan) changes a little each time when an extra word-brick is added:

Boys are bullies.
Big boys are bullies.
Those big boys are bullies.
Some of those big boys are bullies.

Try to say what extra things we know from the extra word-bricks added each time.

Make up a set of four sentences, adding one extra word-brick each time so that the whole meaning plan changes.

2 Try saying these sentences out loud in the *ordinary, natural* way you might say them to someone else:

– It's a **nice** day today, isn't it?
– What a **nice** story!
– Very **nice** of him, I don't think!
– You'll be **nice** and sick after all that ice cream.

You see the word-brick 'nice' comes up in each sentence. Think up different, *ordinary* ways of saying the same things and make sure that you change the word 'nice' each time.

3 Borrow as many different *phrase books* of different languages as you can. Ask your friends or teachers, or look in the libraries near you. Use these phrase books to find out how people say these ideas to each other in different languages:

(a) How are you?
(b) Cheers!
(c) I love you.

Copy down the exact words they would *write* and try to learn how to *say* these words properly. You will find that the same ideas can use completely different spoken and written words.

4 Here are some English 'language-walls' built with big and difficult words, but their meaning plan is in fact quite simple, and you could build the same plan with shorter, easier words. Use a dictionary to find out what these words *mean*, and then build the same plan with easier words. Make sure you don't change the ideas in the meaning plan at all.

(a) The inhalation of smoke may have deleterious effects upon one's health.
(b) An excessive consumption of alcoholic beverages leads to a loss of sobriety.
(c) 'Circumvention or contravention of the regulations of this establishment of learning is unwise,' he said.

THE FINISHING TOUCHES

Tone of voice

When we speak English, we change our tone of voice to give a special kind of meaning to what we are saying. We can use the same speaking plan, with the same word-bricks, and then show the exact idea of our meaning plan by our tone of voice. You can think of this as one of the 'finishing touches' to the language-house: it is like putting doors and windows and furniture into a house. It makes what you say easier for other people to understand. It shows what mood you are in and what your feelings are about what you are saying, so it is a very useful and important part of your language.

Activity 1

Look at the words of this sentence, and try to say them in the different ways suggested. You will need to try out your tone of voice for each one three or four times to get it just right.

'What are you doing in here?'

You could say these words:

Angrily, as if you were annoyed:

It is the word 'are' that is loudest and your voice will go down on the word 'here'.

As a **question**, as if you were just interested. The word 'what' will be the most important one now and your voice will go up on the word 'here'.

In a **bored** way, as if you are not really interested but you thought you should ask. There would not be much change in your tone of voice this time. It would be quite flat and none of the words would seem very important.

47

In a **surprised** way, as if you had not expected to see the other person. The word **'you'** would be loudest now, and your voice would go down on the last few words.

Now try out the same four tones of voice (**angry, interested question, bored** and **surprised**) on a different sentence. Listen to the different meaning that the same words can have each time. Here is the new sentence:

'What's Batman up to now?'

You will find that the way your voice goes up or down at the ends of sentences has to change a little to show the right mood and meaning, and that it is not always the same word that is the loudest.

You can think of these changes as being like the tune of a song. If you just *said* the words of a song they would mean something and other people could understand them. But when the *tune* is added to the same words, they *turn* into a song, they come to life. The language we use every day in English is exactly like that. It would be very dull if we all went around talking to each other without changing our tone of voice – without a 'tune' in our words.

Activity 2

Here's a short act for you to practise. Take one part each with a partner, and practise saying the whole conversation *without changing your tone of voice at all*. There should be no 'tune' in your words. They should be as flat and boring as possible. This is difficult for us to do properly.

Mykot: Hello, Radan. I haven't seen you around lately.

Radan: Hello there, Mykot. You're right. I've been away for the usual check-up.

Mykot: Have you? I'm going for mine next week. How are you feeling?

Radan: Very good, very good indeed. I'm like a new robot.

Mykot: You are looking fine, I must say.

Radan: I got all squeaky and stiff, but there's nothing like a drop of oil.

Mykot: I know. I can't wait. It really puts things right, doesn't it?

Radan: And they re-wired my head a bit too.

Mykot: Very nice it looks too. Very handsome.

Radan: They might fix yours if you ask them. You need it!

48

When you say your part completely without any 'tune', it doesn't sound at all like the normal way English people speak, does it? Now try to say your act, with your partner, in the ordinary way you would speak, giving it all the ordinary tunes that you would use. Make your language as 'natural' as possible. It sounds quite different, doesn't it?

We all speak with 'tunes' in our words. Try listening to some of the everyday tunes that you hear at the dinner table, in the playground, in the shops or on the television. Remember, it is not the words you are going to listen to, but the *tune*. You will hear that the tune has a message of its own. It may tell you things about the way someone else feels – whether he or she feels angry, interested, bored, or surprised, for example.

Activity 3

Here are some groups of words for you to practise different tones of voice with different tunes:

Question tunes
The horse kicked her, did it.
Lend us your bike, will you.
Where's all that jelly gone.
Have you seen my hedgehog anywhere.
Why did you push him down the stairs.
Did he really say that.
How many marbles are there in this jar.

Command tunes
Get on with your homework.
Don't forget the jelly-babies.
Give her that doughnut.
Find that drawing-pin quickly.
Sit down immediately.
Just wait a while.
Bring me a drink.

Surprised tunes
What's he doing here.
I'd never have thought it.
Well, I never.
A hat-trick.
You mean, he won it.
What a thing.
That's incredible.

All of the tunes you will have made here for questions or commands or surprise are different from each other in little ways. And there are hundreds of other different tunes which go with all the different speaking plans and meaning plans that you use every day.

Tunes in other languages

You must remember that English is not the only language in which tunes are an important part of the way you finish off your language-buildings. Other languages have tunes too. You may not know their tunes, and they may take a little time for you to understand, but they are still there, and can be very useful for you to listen to and learn.

49

Here are some nonsense sentences, made up with nonsense words that don't come from any language at all. Perhaps they come from Mars? Take each sentence and give it a tune (a bored or angry or surprised tune, maybe). Practise saying it with exactly the same tune each time, and then ask a friend to say whether he thinks your tune is 'angry' or 'bored' or an 'interested question' or anything else.

Groot snorry blutt, foddle tride.

Ooo frabjuss jabberwock, calloo callay.

Gribble er tozz. Glimp. Bink.

Habble smabble.

Quonk drombie flanter jong.

Sarodlopple.

And now, here are some words from other, real languages, where you should use an **annoyed tune** (where your voice drops from high to low):

Verflucht!   Blast! (German)
(fair-**floocht**) (*ch* as in 'loch')

Zut!   Blast! (French)
(tseet)

Mama mia!   My goodness! (Italian)
(ma-mă **mee**-ă)

Gwarchod pawb!   My goodness! (Welsh)
(gw**ahr**-*ch*od powb) (*ch* as in 'loch')

Try to sound really annoyed when you say these words. Think how dull what you are saying might be if you completely took the tunes away, and spoke like the robots.

Now try to use a **question tune** (where your voice goes up quickly) on these foreign question words:

Alors?   Well then? (*French*)
(a-**lawr**)

Ja?   Yes? (is that so?) (*German*)
(yar)

Bitte?   Sorry? (I didn't hear you) (*German*)
(**bit**-tĕ)

Señor?   Yes, sir? (*Spanish*)
(sen-**yawr**)

Algo más?   Anything else? (*Spanish*)
(**al**-goh mahss)

You can easily hear the tune in these words, can't you? You must remember that longer tunes are used and can be heard in longer sentences too, and they may give you a clue about the way someone else is feeling, even if you cannot understand all the words in the sentence. The tune can sometimes give you a clue about the meaning plan, and from that you may be able to understand the word-bricks and the speaking plan as well.

Getting your accent right

When you have finished building a house, you start to think about the paints and colours that you want for each room. In a language-house, the accent that you speak with is rather like the colours of paint that you might choose in a real house. It is important that the 'colour' of your accent is well-chosen and properly used in your language-house. If the 'colour' of your accent in French or German or *any* foreign language is wrong, then the whole language-house is made uncomfortable for the people who will hear you speak and who will want to understand what you say.

In English we have lots of different kinds of accents: northern English, Cockney, B.B.C., American, Scottish, and so on. All of these are perfectly good English accents – we can't really say that any one of them is the 'right' accent in English. But we do say that foreigners like Italians or Germans or Russians, for example, have a 'foreign' accent. This means that they don't use any one of the real *English* kinds of accent: their mouth-machines don't make real English sounds quite properly. That is what a 'foreign' accent is.

When it comes to *you* learning a foreign language, you have to make sure that you learn one of the *real* accents of that language, which will make you sound exactly like a Frenchman speaking French or a Spaniard speaking Spanish, or whatever . . . Not only does the 'right' accent make you sound *real* in the foreign language, but it will also in the end make that language easier to use and learn.

So how do you learn to have a *real* accent? The answer is: by listening very carefully to the way any new words should be made with your mouth-machine and by trying to make them exactly right yourself. You will be asked to listen to recordings of foreigners saying things in their own language, or to the way your teacher makes the foreign sounds. Then you have to try to copy the same sounds and try to use your mouth-machine in exactly the same way. Slowly but surely, the words you make will sound 'real'.

Activity 5

In English you can see just how important it is to have the right way of saying words (the right way of using your mouth-machine) by looking at these pairs of words. Try to say what the difference is between the words in each pair in:
(a) spelling (the way you write it)
(b) sound (the way your mouth-machine makes it)
(c) meaning (your ideas)

There may not be any difference in either spelling or sound, but there will always be a difference in meaning.

> I think you should *meet* James Bond.
> Tigers eat plenty of *meat*.

> That's *enough*, thanks.
> This hill makes me *puff* and blow.

> I saw a *bear* in the forest.
> I can't *bear* spinach.

> I can easily *read* this book.
> I have already *read* this book.

> The *wolf* saw the lambs and licked his lips.
> *Golf* is a very difficult sport.

> You can *see* the *sea* from the top of this hill.

> We had seats in the first *row*.
> They were having a terrible *row*.

Now if you think how difficult it would be for us to understand a foreigner speaking English who got these sounds muddled up, you will see how *you* could easily muddle up sounds in a foreign language by not making them the right way.

Have you heard the joke about the message that was sent through from France during the war by an English army officer? He wrote 'Germans advancing on West Bank. Please send more men'. The message went through a French army radio-post to London. When the message arrived there, it read:

'Germans are dancing on wet plank. Please send four hens'.

The message was useless. One of the French radio operators had not got his accent quite right.

Activity 6

Tongue-twisters can be used to practise the way you make certain sounds. First try these English ones as fast as possible.

(a) Around the rugged rocks the ragged rascal ran.

(b) If Peter Piper picked a peck of pickled peppers
How many pecks of pickled peppers did Peter Piper pick?

(c) How much wood would a woodpecker peck
If a woodpecker would peck wood?
As much wood as a woodpecker would peck
If a woodpecker would peck wood.

(d) The Leith police dismisseth us.

If you don't get your pronunciation exactly right here, you end up tripping over the words. An accent in a foreign language works in the same sort of way – if you make one sound wrong, the other sounds are more difficult to make properly too. Try these two German tongue-twisters, slowly at first and then more quickly. Follow the pronunciation guide underneath each word to get the sounds right:

(a) In Ulm um Ulm um Ulm herum.
(in uulm uum uulm uum uulm hair-**uum**)

(b) Fritz Fischer fischt frische Fische.
(frits **fish**-er fisht **frish**-ĕ **fish**-ĕ)

When you start practising saying whole sentences in other languages, you may find they are rather like these tongue-twisters. The thing to remember is to get your accent right, and to make it sound as *real* and as 'comfortable' for other people as you can.

Polite language, rude language

Buildings are designed and built for particular reasons in particular places. If the building is put in the wrong place people will not like it or want to live in it. Language-buildings are just the same: if the wrong thing is said at the wrong time and place, it will not be useful or pleasant for other people. We all have to learn *when* and *where* and *how* to say things in our own language, and in other languages too. That is what makes the difference between 'polite' language and 'rude' language.

Most of us swear and use 'bad' language in English at some time or another. People who speak other languages do just the same thing. Words can be used like shades of paint: bright or dark colours? pale tones or sharp tones? Choosing the right sort of words to suit a particular time or place or person is like choosing the right colour to suit your house. You speak to your friends in a slightly different way than you speak to your teacher or your parents or to a stranger, for example. If your headmaster knocked you over in the street by mistake you might be a bit more polite with your words than if your brother had done it. And yet all the words that you *could* use at a moment like that are part of the same language – they are all part of the English language. You choose one of them instead of the other to fit the place and the people who can hear you.

It's not only swearing or slang that work like that. You change your language in all sorts of other ways too. You may 'put on' a 'posh' accent (making 'posh' English sounds with your mouth-machine), or you may use slightly different speaking plans or maybe sometimes you would use a different tone of voice with a different 'tune'.

Look at these two sentences:

To a stranger:

To a good friend:

You can easily see which one of the two sentences is trying to be more 'polite'.

And then what about these sentences? You should be able to say which one is more 'polite' straight away, even though you are really saying the same thing in both of them.

'E's nicked me book!'

or 'He's stolen my book, sir!'

'I wonder whether you could help me?'

or 'Give us a hand, will you?'

You see, the language you use has just changed slightly to suit the place and the person in each one of these sentences.

Activity 7

Here are a few more words or expressions that you might hear in one place rather than another, or with one sort of person speaking rather than another. The language suits the place – but what kind of places are these and who do you think is speaking?

1 I declare you man and wife.
2 Stand at ease!
3 British Rail apologizes to passengers for the delays in their services to Scotland.
4 Och, the wee bairn didna ken.

53

5 Blimey, Conteh's right hook is like a hammer, isn't it?

6 I hereby sentence you to a term of imprisonment of not less than five years.

7 Open your books at page 10, please . . . Jeremy, stop talking!

8 And that's the end of the news.

You should have been able to work out *where* you might hear language like this just from the words themselves. If you were helped by hearing the accent and the tune that might go with them, you would of course find it even easier to tell.

Activity 8	

You can say exactly the same sort of thing and give the same sort of message to different people in different ways. Work out the different ways you would tell
(a) your headmaster
(b) your parents
(c) your best friend
about this piece of news:

> A small boy in your school has sworn at a bigger boy and the bigger boy has hit him round the ear. He has knocked him out.

Keep the news short and to the point each time. Would you use exactly the same words to tell all three different people about it? See what differences there are and make sure you use the *real* language that you know you would use.

When you come to learn a foreign language you will find, later on, that some words suit certain places and people and not others, just as they do in English. In French, for example, the word for 'a boy' is 'un garçon', but when talking to your friends you might use the word 'un mec' instead; and you might call a girl 'une nana' instead of 'une jeune fille'. If you made a mistake and used these words in the wrong situation, you wouldn't be using 'rude' language, but people would know that you couldn't use their language properly yet.

Talking with your face and hands

We all sometimes 'talk' to each other without actually *saying* anything – we send messages by smiling, waving, grinning, winking, or shrugging our shoulders. This is all part of the extra 'furniture' that we can put into our language-houses to make them more comfortable, more easy for other people to understand. We send extra messages with the expression on our faces or by moving our hands – we have already seen how deaf and dumb people use these two ways of making up *everything* that they say to each other.

Think how difficult it would be if we didn't all use the same signals with our faces or hands or shoulders to say 'I don't know' (a shrug) or 'How nice to see you' (a smile). All dogs wag their tails instead of smiling, but we haven't got tails any more, so we smile or we shake hands.

But not all countries *do* use the same signals. When we say 'yes', we may nod our heads, and to say 'no' we may shake our heads. But in Bulgaria, one of the countries of south-eastern Europe, people do it the other way round. To say 'yes' they *shake* their heads and to say 'no' they *nod*.

Activity 9

Work with a friend here. One of you should ask these questions and the other one should try answering them just by using the Bulgarian way of *nodding* to say 'no' and *shaking your head* to say 'yes'. You must also *say* 'yes' or 'no' out loud at the same time. See how many mistakes you make out of the ten answers.

1 Do you like spaghetti and tomato sauce?
2 Have cats got tails?
3 Is your teacher nice to you?
4 Do you watch too much television?
5 Have you got any brothers or sisters?
6 Do you like playing football?
7 Have you ever been to France?
8 Do you like school?
9 Are you good at adding up?
10 Is ice cream your favourite food?

You will probably have found it difficult not to use the English nodding and shaking signals for 'yes' and 'no'.

So you can see that not everyone uses signals with their hands or faces in exactly the same way all over the world. When you learn another language you have to try to use hand- and face-signals in the right way to fit that language. The French and Italians and Spanish wave their hands about more than we do when they are talking, for example, to add extra signals to what they are saying, as if they want to make their arms speak for them too!

Activity 10

These are some things that you would often say by a look on your face or a simple signal with your shoulders or hands. Try to make the *ordinary signals* for these ideas, without saying anything at all out loud!

1 I haven't got a clue.
2 Come over here.
3 Be quiet, don't talk!
4 Pooh! what a stink!
5 Yes, I know the answer, miss!
8 Bye bye!
6 He's crazy.
7 I'm starving hungry.
9 Oh dear, I feel really fed up.
10 Yes, that's right
11 It's terrible
12 Speak a bit louder.
13 Come on! I'm waiting.
14 Let's all hope so.

You see, there are a whole lot of things that we 'say' to each other without actually using words. Keep your eyes open when you are learning a new language, as well as your ears – you will pick up a lot of extra, helpful clues about meaning plans and word-bricks especially.

55

Things to discover

1 Borrow a small tape-recorder with a microphone and a blank tape. Use it to record two different people reading the same short piece of a book or comic for you. Try to find people who you know come from different countries or different parts of England. Then listen to the recording again and try to find any differences between the two recordings. Listen for differences in:

(a) their *tunes*: rises and falls in their voices.

(b) their *accents*: the ways they made the words with their mouth-machines.

2 Use a transistor radio, and tune in to a French or German radio station. Listen carefully to the people speaking for a few minutes. Then try to say when you think the French or German people speaking are

(a) asking questions
(b) giving answers
(c) surprised
(d) angry
(e) pleased.

Try to say *why* you think it. What are the clues you have used? If you can't find a good radio station to listen to, ask your teacher to borrow a tape-recording of some French or German people speaking, instead.

3 How do people who come from the Manchester or Liverpool area of England say these words:

bus, bath, cook, that, shoe, some, under, honest?

Their English accent is different from the English accent you hear, for example, on the radio or television news. Try to say which parts of the words they make differently – what their difference in accent is in these words.

4 Collect photos from home or from magazines and newspapers which show some *groups* of three or four people. Now, for each photo, try to think what these people might be saying to each other. What are they doing? Why? So what do they say?

Give each person in the photo a name and write down a short play which shows what they were saying to each other. It should look something like this:

Name A: Borgle sned, yorra.
Name B: Gurness.
Name C: Guiness?
Name D: Drib! Gurness!

But not like that! Write *real* words.

USING YOUR LANGUAGES

Why learn languages?

People build houses for a special reason – they want to live in them. They build shops to buy and sell food or clothes in; they build factories to work in and school-buildings to learn in and cinemas to see films in. All these buildings are planned, built, and finished to fit the needs of the people who will use them.

Language-building is just the same. A language is learned, practised, and then tried out to make sure that it can really be *used* in a foreign country, to talk to foreign people who may not be able to speak any English.

When you start learning a new language you will want to listen to how the word-bricks are made with your mouth-machine, how they are used in meaning plans, how different speaking plans can be made and used, and so on. You will want to see and hear how their language is used by the people who can already speak it properly.

The aim of this book is to help you to enjoy looking at the way your new second language is made, and to look at the way English, your own language, is made. They are both built up with interesting kinds of plans and tools and materials. They look different and they sound different maybe, but they are both language-houses.

But *why* will you want to see or hear how the new language works or how it is used? Well, people all have different reasons for learning new languages, but the main reason is so that they can speak to each other easily and find out about each other's lives and ideas. You will be able to talk to foreign people about their countries, listen to their radio, read their newspapers, watch their television, find your way around the place on your own, and so on. For example, you would be in trouble if you didn't know how to ask where the toilet was in France or Spain or Germany, wouldn't you?

Or what about finding somewhere to have a meal? Or buying a bus ticket? These are only a few of the ways in which speaking and understanding a foreign language properly will be useful to you.

We started out at the beginning of this book thinking about all the thousands of languages that people are using *now*, as you read, all over the world. They are still there, talking and listening to each other. It's time you joined them . . .

The last activity

Your last activity will never end. You will always be learning new language. That new language may be more and more English – new words or ways of saying things to people in your own language. Or it may be new words and ways of saying things to people in *their* foreign languages. You never stop learning language. So here is something for you to start off with: find out what these languages are, how to *say* these sentences properly, and roughly what they mean. You can get help from anywhere.

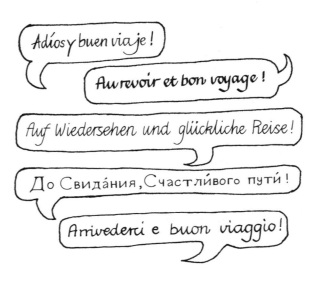

ANSWERS

Unit 1

Activity 5
theatre, soldier, officer, general, mutton (sheep), duke, chair, chimney, palace, beef

apple, beer, man, number, market, leather, thing, bread, chocolate, paper

Activity 6
1 'Red' Indian languages: North America
2 Russian, Russia
3 Italian, Italy
4 German, Germany
5 Greek, Greece
6 Spanish, Spain and Mexico
7 Japanese, Japan
8 Arabic, Arabia and North Africa

Things to discover
2 Dutch, Spanish, French/German/Italian, French/English, Hebrew
3 (a) At least 3,000–4,000.
  (b) Teeth and roof of mouth; lips and tongue.
  (c) English and French both belong to the Indo-European family.
  (d) Norman Conquest by William the Conqueror in 1066.

Unit 2

Activity 1
'Do not walk on the grass'
(1) do (2) not (3) walk (4) on (5) the (6) grass
'Opening hours'
(1) open (2) -ing (3) hour (4) -s
'Waiting room'
(1) wait (2) -ing (3) room
'I don't really know'
(1) I (2) do (3) -n't (4) real (5) -ly (6) know

Activity 2
Penguin, -s, elephant, go, -ing, and, their, trunk, in, the, do, -er, to, they, swim, long

Activity 3
English:	French:
1 re-	1 étrange-
2 dis-, believe, -er	2 -ère
3 un-, -ed, -ly	3 -esse
4 pay, re-, -ment, -able	4 dé-, -re, -er
5 less, -er	5 re-, -er
6 -berry, black-, -est	6 in-, -ble

Activity 4
1 Fussball = football
2 Krankenschwester = nurse
3 Kartoffelsuppe = potato soup
4 fünfundzwanzig = twenty-five
5 Zahnbürste = toothbrush
6 Butterbrot = bread and butter/sandwich
7 Frühstück = breakfast
8 Fernsprecher = telephone

Activity 5
Masculine words: alumno, mozo, novio, libro, perro, helado, vino

Feminine words: alumna, moza, novia, libra, pera, naranja, manzana

Activity 6
English: knives, children, hoofs/hooves, wives, oxen, mice, sheep, goldfish, geese
Spanish: (a) chicos, casas, mesas, sombreros
(b) futboles, panes, soles, revólveres

Things to discover
4 A.A. Automobile Association
R.A.F. Royal Air Force
F.A. Football Association
B.R. British Rail
H.M. Her/His Majesty
G.B. Great Britain
I.R.A. Irish Republican Army
K.K.K. Ku Klux Klan
U.S.S.R. Union of Soviet Socialist Republics

5 (a) buzzing   (f) buzzing
     (b) hissing   (g) hissing
     (c) buzzing   (h) 'siz'
     (d) hissing   (i) buzzing
     (e) hissing   (j) hissing

Unit 3

Activity 1

1 God save the Queen!
2 Once upon a time, . . .
3 Two and two make four.
4 I am reading my comic.
5 You look like a hot dog!
6 Could you pass the salt please?/Please could you . . .
7 I think Elvis is the greatest.
8 Teachers are not always horrible.
9 The Sahara desert is very hot.
10 Marmite comes in small brown jars.

Activity 3

1 | They | like | toast | and | jam | (one less brick)
or | They | do | like | toast | and | jam | (same number)

2 | That | big | boy | is | a | bully | (same number)

3 | This | little | girl | is | clever | (same number)

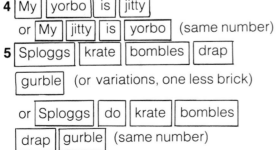

4 | My | yorbo | is | jitty |
or | My | jitty | is | yorbo | (same number)

5 | Sploggs | krate | bombles | drap |
| gurble | (or variations, one less brick)
or | Sploggs | do | krate | bombles |
| drap | gurble | (same number)

Activity 4

Gaston: I am terribly hungry. I am twelve years old. It is very warm today, isn't it? I am wearing a black hat and a red tie.

Gustav: Have you made the coffee already? I will go to London by train at two o'clock. I like eating everything I can see. I have no more money because I have spent it all (everything).

Activity 5

1 Frogs eat flies *and spiders*/Frogs *and spiders* eat flies.
Frogs *like to* eat flies . . .
Green frogs like to . . .
Some green frogs like to . . . (or sensible alternatives)

2 Comics are *very* boring.
Comics are *not* very boring.
Most comics are . . .
Most *American* comics are . . .
Most American comics *and films* are . . .

3 Are *those* comics boring?
Are*n't* those . . . ?
Why aren't those . . . ?
Why aren't those *war* comics . . . ?
Why aren't those *old* war . . . ?
Why aren't those old *torn* war . . . ?

4 Judy *kicked and* hit Punch.
Judy kicked and hit *poor* Punch.
Ugly Judy kicked . . .
Ugly *old* Judy/. . . poor *old* Punch.
Ugly old Judy kicked and hit poor old Punch *on the nose*.

Activity 6

French language-wall:
(a) jaune (b) vraie (c) petit (d) et noir (e) tropicale

German language-wall:
(a) und dem grünen Haar (b) sehr (c) mit dem roten Gesicht (d) und schöne (e) junge (f) alte

Things to discover

2 (a) Imperative   (f) Negative
     (b) Interrogative   (g) Imperative
     (c) Interrogative   (h) Interrogative
     (d) Negative   (i) Negative
     (e) Imperative   (j) Interrogative

3 (a) Fred is a good bloke.
     (b) He likes football.
     (c) He watches matches.
     (d) He supports Liverpool.

(e) Liverpool are great.
(f) They won the Cup.
(g) I support Liverpool.
(h) They are my favourite team.
(i) Fred is my best friend.

Beginning of sentences: capital letters
End of sentences: full stops

Unit 4

Activity 1
Possible answers:
1 elephant
2 camera
3 frying pan?/saucepan?
4 dog?/poodle?
5 ? (close-up of bristles of brush)
6 ? (head of a beetle)

Activity 4
Some possible answers:
1 (a) chicken   hungry
   (b) sunshine/sunny
        swimming/swimming-pool
   (c) music/rock/guitarist
        dance/dancing/disco
   (d) dog
        tele/the box etc.
   (e) elephant
        ant
        flowers
2 Any sensible alternatives to the
  suggestions above.
3 Any sensible, real English sentences
  using the words thought of.
4 Different real sentences using the same
  words.

Activity 5
The picture: Two faces and a cup/goblet

1 a river (runs)
2 a clock (hands)
3 a comb (teeth)
4 Push it. (roll)
5 Because their horns don't work.
6 a taxi-driver (drives)
7 a cannibal (fed up)
8 'wrong' (right/wrong)

Activity 6
1 Simba = lion (mane . . . roared . . .
  hunted)
2 chui = leopard (spotted coat . . . claws
  . . . antelope for supper)
3 tembo = elephant (trunk . . . huge back)
4 samaki = fish (jump out of water . . .
  scales . . . silver)
5 tumbili = monkey (orange in his hand . . .
  tail)

Activity 7
1 bottiglia – bottle
  birra – beer
  Is that a bottle of beer?
2 bouteille – bottle
  bière – beer
  Yes, it's a bottle of beer.
3 hier – here, alt – old, Buch – book
  Here is your old book.
4 diccionario – dictionary, no – not, mío
  – (me) mine.
  This dictionary isn't mine.
5 oncle – uncle, stupide – stupid
  My uncle is stupid.
6 mein – my, Bruder – brother, dumm –
  (dumb) stupid
  And my brother is stupid.

Unit 5

Activity 7
1 A vicar, at a wedding
2 A sergeant-major, in the army, on parade
3 A station-master, at the railway-station
4 A Scotsman or Scotswoman (no
  particular place)
5 A sports fan at a boxing-match
6 A judge, in the courtroom
7 A teacher in a classroom, starting a
  lesson
8 A newsreader on radio or television

Activity 10
1 'I haven't got a clue' – shrug your
  shoulders.
2 'Come over here' – crook your finger.
3 'Be quiet, don't talk' – put your first
  finger across your lips.

4 'Pooh! what a stink!' – hold your nose with your thumb and finger.

5 'Yes, I know the answer, miss' – put your hand and arm up.

6 'He's crazy' – tap the side of your head with your finger.

7 'I'm starving hungry' – rub your belly with your hand.

8 'Bye bye!' – wave your hand.

9 'Oh dear, I feel fed up' – pull the corners of your mouth down.

10 'Yes, that's right' – thumbs up, or nod.

11 'It's terrible' – thumbs down.

12 'Speak a bit louder' – put your cupped hand behind your ear.

13 'Come on! I'm waiting' – yawn, drum fingers on table, hands on hips and impatient look on your face.

14 'Let's all hope so' – fingers crossed.

Unit 6

The last activity
Goodbye and have a good journey!

Spanish (a-dee-**oss** ee **bwen** vee-ah-*ch*eh) (*ch* as in 'loch')

French (oh rĕ-**vwar** ay bon vwy-**ahj**)

German (owf **vee**-der-zay-ĕn oont **glook**-li-*ch*ĕ **ry**-zĕ) (*ch* as in 'loch')

Russian (doh svee-**dah**-nya, schah-**stlee**-voh-goh poo-**tee**)

Italian (a-ree-vĕ-**der**-chi ay **bwon** vi-**a**-jee-oh)